THE other AMERICA

Teens & DEPRESSION

by
Gail B. Stewart

Photographs by
Theodore E. Roseen

Lucent Books, P.O. Box 289011, San Diego, CA 92198-9011

These and other titles are included in *The Other America* series:

Battered Women	People with AIDS
The Elderly	Teen Fathers
Gangs	Teen Mothers
Gay and Lesbian Youth	Teen Runaways
The Homeless	Teens and Depression
Illegal Immigrants	Teens in Prison
Mothers on Welfare	

Cover design: Carl Franzen

Library of Congress Cataloging-in-Publication Data

Stewart, Gail 1949–
 Teens & depression / by Gail B. Stewart ; photographs by Theodore
E. Roseen.
  p. cm. — (The other America)
 Includes bibliographical references and index.
 Summary: Text and first-person accounts present the experiences of
teenagers who have coped with and tried to overcome depression.
 ISBN 1-56006-577-X (alk. paper)
 1. Depression in adolescence—Juvenile literature. [1. Depression,
Mental.] I. Roseen, Theodore, E., 1975–   ill. II. Title. III. Series:
Stewart, Gail, 1949–   Other America.
RJ506.D4S74   1998
616.85′27′00835—dc21   97–37735
                                                           CIP
                                                            AC

Printed in the U.S.A.
Copyright © 1998 by Lucent Books, Inc.
P.O. Box 289011, San Diego, CA 92198-9011

Contents

Foreword

O, YES,
I SAY IT PLAIN,
AMERICA NEVER WAS AMERICA TO ME.
AND YET I SWEAR THIS OATH—
AMERICA WILL BE!
    LANGSTON HUGHES

Perhaps more than any other nation in the world, the United States represents an ideal to many people. The ideal of equality—of opportunity, of legal rights, of protection against discrimination and oppression. To a certain extent, this image has proven accurate. But beneath this ideal lies a less idealistic fact—many segments of our society do not feel included in this vision of America.

They are the outsiders—the homeless, the elderly, people with AIDS, teenage mothers, gang members, prisoners, and countless others. When politicians and the media discuss society's ills, the members of these groups are defined as what's wrong with America; they are the people who need fixing, who need help, or increasingly, who need to take more responsibility. And as these people become society's fix-it problem, they lose all identity as individuals and become part of an anonymous group. In the media and in our minds these groups are identified by condition—a disease, crime, morality, poverty. Their condition becomes their identity, and once this occurs, in the eyes of society, they lose their humanity.

The Other America series reveals the members of these groups as individuals. Through in-depth interviews, each person tells his or her unique story. At times these stories are painful, revealing individuals who are struggling to maintain their integrity, their humanity, their lives, in the face of fear, loss, and economic and spiritual hardship. At other times, their tales are exasperating, demonstrating a litany of poor choices, shortsighted thinking, and self-gratification. Nevertheless, their identities remain distinct, their personalities diverse.

As we listen to the people of *The Other America* series describe their experiences they cease to be stereotypically defined and become tangible, individual. In the process, we may begin to understand more profoundly and think more critically about society's problems. When politicians debate, for example, whether the homeless problem is due to a poor economy or lack of initiative, it will help to read the words of the homeless. Perhaps then we can see the issue more clearly. The family who finds itself temporarily homeless because it has always been one paycheck from poverty is not the same as the mother of six who has been chronically chemically dependent. These people's circumstances are not all of one kind, and perhaps we, after all, are not so very different from them. Before we can act to solve the problems of the Other America, we must be willing to look down their path, to see their faces. And perhaps in doing so, we may find a piece of ourselves as well.

Introduction

THE FACTS ABOUT TEENS AND DEPRESSION

Thomas* is a thirteen-year-old who, up until two months ago, was a straight-A student in junior high school. He played soccer on a traveling team, and was popular with his classmates and teachers. Today, however, he is obviously troubled. No emotion or enthusiasm exists in his voice, and his face is a mask of indifference. He rarely looks at his schoolwork; he is failing most of his classes. He quit the soccer team and instead spends afternoons in his room sleeping.

At sixteen Carolyn is a loner. She spends a lot of time thinking about killing herself, and has attempted it once by taking an overdose of her mother's sleeping pills. Carolyn has experimented with acid and pot, and drinks whenever she can acquire liquor.

Mickey is fifteen and has learning disabilities that make school difficult for him. His teachers try to give him the extra help he needs, but he is often unruly and uncooperative in class. Mickey is irritable with his fellow students, too, and has started fights with other boys in school. He has been suspended twice as a result. His loud, obnoxious behavior continues, although the principal has threatened him with expulsion if things do not improve.

While their symptoms may seem different, these three teens are all suffering from clinical depression, a disorder that affects as many as six million children under the age of eighteen, the vast majority of them in their teens. Psychologists believe that tens of thousands more cases of teen depression are untreated and unreported. The results of such depression vary widely. Some depressed teens show a marked loss of interest in friends or activities they once found pleasurable. Many refuse to go to school or, if they do go, they do poorly. Some initiate fights and cause se-

---

* The names of the teens mentioned in this introduction have been changed to protect their privacy.

vere tension within their families. And some, sadly, exhibit self-destructive behavior—even suicide.

WHAT IS CLINICAL DEPRESSION?

Mental health experts say bouts of depression are common. At times everyone feels down or discouraged; even very young children can experience feelings of depression. Sometimes the cause of a teen's depression is obvious: the death of a grandparent, poor performance on a test in school, breaking up with a girlfriend or boyfriend. Usually the sadness and "down-in-the-dumps" feeling goes away in a few days.

Sometimes, however, depression seems to come out of nowhere, with no apparent reasons. A teen feels so irritable or sad that nothing makes her feel better, and the depression continues for weeks or even months. When this happens, the depression interferes with a teen's ability to function at school, at home, and with her peers. This kind of depression is called *clinical depression* by professionals, and can be diagnosed when someone exhibits five or more of the following symptoms (not related to any medical condition or drugs) during a two-week period, according to the American Psychiatric Association:

1. a depressed mood most of the day, nearly every day.
2. markedly diminished interest or pleasure in most activity during the day, nearly every day.
3. significant weight loss or gain over a month (for instance, a change of more than 5 percent of body weight).
4. significant change in sleep habits—sleeping far more or far less than usual.
5. extreme agitation or extreme slowness of movement nearly every day.
6. fatigue or loss of energy nearly every day.
7. feelings of worthlessness or excessive guilt every day.
8. diminished ability to concentrate, or indecisiveness nearly every day.
9. recurrent thoughts of death or suicide (or suicide attempts).

Special help is needed to cure a teen's clinical depression, for although episodes may lessen over extended periods of time, there is a danger of suicide if the teen's depression becomes too severe. Help for clinical depression can range from help from the teen's parents and family members to counseling and therapy, often combined with certain medications. In certain cases in which the teen is a danger to himself, hospitalization is used until the crisis has passed.

Although a great deal still needs to be learned about the causes of clinical depression, many psychiatrists believe that it is caused by an abnormal kind of chemical activity in the brain. Brain cells communicate with one another by releasing chemicals called neurotransmitters. During depression, these neurotransmitters become underactive, interfering with the body's normal rhythms. When this happens, it is believed, loss of energy, hopelessness, and feelings of sadness begin.

NOT A CAREFREE TIME

Depression in young people was not recognized as a disorder until the 1970s. Before, psychologists dismissed the idea of sadness or prolonged feelings of despair in children and teens.

"Youth and childhood were supposed to be the carefree times," says Penny Enderly, a child therapist who specializes in depression. "Psychiatrists then believed that children led G-rated lives, with blue skies, flowers, balloons, and puppies. They bought into the myth that because of their innocence and their youth, kids could not feel anguish and depression. They simply denied the existence of those conditions.

"Of course, now we know that that simply isn't true. Kids have lots of stress in their lives, too; they worry about a lot of things their parents worry about—divorce, death, money—in addition to their own problems. Besides the children from seemingly functional families, many children and adolescents live X-rated lives. They are living in homes where violence, drugs, sexual or emotional abuse are all a part of daily life. And serious depression in many of these children is all too common."

THE MASKS OF DEPRESSION

Depression in adults is fairly easy for a psychologist to diagnose. Adults often verbalize their feelings of sadness or anxiety; they act as though they are tired, and they seem unenthusiastic. Young people, however, often mask their depression, expressing it in far different ways than adults.

Sometimes teens constantly complain that they are bored, even when they are participating in activities they normally enjoy. Some feel fatigued and want to sleep all the time, while others suffer prolonged bouts of insomnia. Teens may also complain of stomachaches, headaches, or other physical maladies. Some become lonely and detached from their family and friends or exhibit signs of eating disorders—rapidly gaining or losing weight.

Such "masks" of depression are troublesome, for they can make it difficult for parents or doctors to understand the true cause of the problem. Often parents and teachers assume that the child is merely going through the moodiness that is common in adolescence, or is coming down with a virus or other infection. Even when parents suspect their child is suffering from a mental illness, they may deny the existence of the depression out of feelings of guilt or embarrassment.

Mental health professionals worry that many depressed teens do not receive the treatment they need. A 1992 survey among 5,320 students in eighth, ninth, and tenth grades reveals, for instance, that 61 percent of the students reported experiencing feelings of depression and hopelessness. An astonishing 34 percent had considered committing suicide, and 14 percent had actually attempted it. According to suicide prevention workers, an estimated 5,000 young people take their lives annually. And for every completed teen suicide, between 50 and 200 attempts are probably made. Most of these attempts are not reported and many go unnoticed by family or friends of the suicidal teen.

Suicide is certainly the final desperate act by a seriously depressed teen, but other self-destructive behavior often precedes suicide attempts. Some teens run away from home, often enduring dangerous conditions while they live on the streets. Some become heavily involved in drugs or alcohol and resort to selling drugs to support their expensive habits.

ANOTHER FORM OF DEPRESSION

Various types and degrees of clinical depression exist, but psychiatrists say bipolar disorder, or manic depression, is becoming more common in teens. Bipolar disorder is almost never seen in children; adults have traditionally suffered this form of depression. Increasingly, however, mental health workers are seeing it in teens—some as young as thirteen or fourteen.

Bipolar disorder differs from regular clinical depression; a person with bipolar disorder has alternating episodes of extremely high and low moods of depression. As with clinical depression, it is believed that the neurotransmitters in the brain are behaving abnormally—in this case, becoming alternately underactive in the depressive stage and overactive in the manic stage. These mood swings can be so abrupt and severe that they can make it almost impossible for a teen to carry on what was his "normal" life.

The signs of bipolar disorder include the same signs of clinical depression, but also several symptoms of the manic phase. These symptoms may include extreme excitement or giddiness; explosive anger; an exaggerated sense of the teen's abilities; rapid, constant speech that is often difficult for others to understand or follow; a huge increase in energy—sometimes the ability to go for many hours without rest; and impulsive, risk-taking behavior, such as reckless driving or excessive drinking.

Although clinical depression, including bipolar disorder, sounds like a problem too frightening and serious for a teen to endure, the prognosis is far from hopeless, say psychologists. The first step is getting professional help from a therapist who can determine the best treatment for the depressed teen.

COUNSELORS, THERAPISTS, AND FAMILY CAN HELP

In the early stages of depression, teens can often be helped by their own families. Counselors and therapists can help parents and siblings understand the best way of coping with a depressed family member. "I was devastated at first when Meghan was diagnosed," says one mother. "Neither her father nor I had any understanding of mental illness. We sort of tiptoed around, not knowing when Meghan would start one of her moods next. But working with an adolescent therapist at our clinic, we had to learn to be more assertive about talking to Meghan—not so 'chicken,' as my husband puts it. We've learned how to talk about things which are bothering her, or bothering us. They're skills we all wish we'd learned a long time ago, but I'm glad we know them now. We're all still learning, and it's not easy. But Meghan is getting to be her old self again, and we're so grateful."

More severe cases may require medications or intense therapy sessions to stabilize the depressed teen's moods. And in extremely severe cases, hospitalization is used to control psychotic or irrational behavior, or to prevent the teen from harming himself or others.

"We've been dealing with our son's behavior for two and a half years," says Bernie's father. "He's been on medication, and he's had some real intensive therapy with a very understanding counselor. We know, and Bernie knows, it will be something he'll probably be dealing with for a long time. But the most important thing is that we all know that there is hope. I can see that now, and two years ago I would never have believed that."

Although stories such as these are optimistic and hopeful, others are not. Not every teen is lucky enough to have understanding parents or a family that can provide support. Psychiatrists say that only 20 percent of teens suffering from clinical depression or bipolar disorder are getting help for their conditions. For many teens, the outlook is not nearly so hopeful.

Four Depressed Teens

In *The Other America: Teens and Depression*, readers will meet young people from a variety of backgrounds. Some have had loving support in their bouts with depression, others have tried dealing with it on their own. There are successes here, as well as failures.

Nathan is a sparkly eyed fourteen-year-old who, although shy about speaking of the sexual abuse he suffered as a preschooler, has found success through the strength of his family. Instead of using traditional medications to treat his depression, Nathan's parents are using homeopathy, an alternative style of medicine. In addition, Nathan has a passionate interest in animals, which as he says, "keeps me thinking about happier things."

Ryan, a fourteen-year-old "throwaway," is one teen who has not had support. His parents are uninterested in him, and his life on the street gives him few chances to seek the therapy he needs.

Nineteen-year-old Runa is a story of hope. From her life with a psychotic mother in a housing project, Runa has battled with suicide attempts, breakdowns, and medications with painful and complicated side effects. She is determined to stay off the medications, pursue a new life as a college student, and keep her depression at bay.

Finally, there is Julia, seventeen, equally pessimistic about her chances to regain control of her life. A teenage mother with an infant daughter, Julia says she cannot remember the last time she was happy. All she has to live for, she admits, is her daughter, and she is fervently hoping that is enough to give her the strength to fight her depression.

Nathan

"SURVIVAL IS CRUCIAL TO ANY
SPECIES, AND I'M SURE . . .
PEOPLE WHO HAVE BEEN HURT
ARE MORE INTO SURVIVAL THAN
THOSE WHO HAVE IT PRETTY
EASY."

*Author's Note: I was introduced to Nathan by his mother, who had told me
that her son had been diagnosed as clinically depressed. Nathan's parents
believe that his depression began when he was four after he was sexually
abused by a nursery school teacher. His mother—quite understandably—
felt very guilty about the fact he was abused, for it was not discovered until
more than a year after it had occurred. For years after the incidents, she
says, she felt terrible that she had continued to drop him off at the preschool
each morning, not knowing then what Nathan was going through once he
got there. Nathan and his parents have undergone therapy to help them
deal with the abuse and its aftereffects. It was at the time of this counseling
that some of Nathan's behavior led his therapist to diagnose him as "clinically depressed." Some of the behaviors he exhibited were threats of killing
himself, uncontrollable rage, excessive tiredness, nervousness, and a lack of
enjoyment in things that normally had been fun for Nathan.*

*Today Nathan is extremely likable; he does not act in ways one would
identify as "depressed." He is talkative, especially about his animals
and his enjoyment of basketball. He readily says that he is close to his
parents—something many fourteen-year-olds are reluctant to do—and
gives the impression that they have created a strong line of communica-
tion. Although Nathan is not as comfortable talking to me about the abuse
as he is about other aspects of his life, he acknowledges that it might have
made him act "kind of strange" when he was younger, although in his
mind, he is no longer suffering any effects of it.*

It's impossible not to like Nathan, a lanky fourteen-year-old with dark brown eyes and a bashful grin. He seems serious and shy at first, but ask him a question about his pets and he begins an animated monologue about tree frogs, skinks, and lizards of all kinds.

"It's called a hairy frog," he says, explaining about a species of frog he read about in a magazine. "In the spring they get really buff in their upper bodies—they get arms like Popeye, you know? It has something to do with attracting other frogs during mating season. And their back legs have tiny pieces of skin that stick out, and fill up with blood, so the skin pieces look like long tufts of hair! It isn't really hair, though, it's just the blood-filled skin pieces that look like hair. They're big, too—I think the author of the article I read said they get between five and six inches long. If they ever became available around here, you bet I'd get one to keep. But I'm sure they're not too easy to come by."

He has run out of information on the Hairy Frog, but that animal reminds him of another animal he would like to see, and his talking continues rapid-fire, almost impossible to interrupt. He can go on for hours, he says with a wry smile, and stops talking—although reluctantly.

DIFFERENT FROM OTHER KIDS

Nathan and his family live in a quiet suburb of the city, with trees and woods and lots of space. He has two younger brothers and a large Saint Bernard named Sheba. With his Nike cap, shorts, and a white oversized T-shirt with "Minnesota Golden Gophers Basketball" emblazoned across the chest, Nathan could be any ninth-grader from any middle class family in Minnesota.

However, says Nathan, he often feels like he is different from other boys his age. He suffers from depression, a condition that can affect people of every age—from adults to very young children. As a result of his depression, Nathan has faced feelings of suicide, hostility, and loneliness. While his interest in animals is pleasurable, it is often not enough to ward off the sadness he sometimes feels.

He has been told by psychologists that he is not alone—millions of children and adolescents in the United States struggle through bouts of severe depression, some of which might last for months or even years. Although there are many kinds of depression, and many factors which can trigger it, Nathan's parents believe his

Although Nathan looks like any boy his age, he says his depression sets him apart from other teens.

depression has been caused in part by a stressful occurrence in his early childhood. Despite his difficulty in speaking about his depression, Nathan has agreed to share his story—one that he hopes will help others his age.

"I DON'T LIKE TO REMEMBER IT"

"I was abused," he starts out, "and it happened when I was just a little kid, about four years old. It was sexual abuse, yeah. I don't like to remember it. I know it happened when we were living in Colorado. My parents both worked, and they took me to a day care there. They'd drop me off in the morning, and pick me up later in the afternoon—it was a place not too far from where we lived.

"There was this one teacher at the day care who I was really afraid of. His name was Dale, and he had blond hair and a mustache. He yelled a lot at the kids, especially the boys. I remember mostly that he played favorites, you know what I mean? Like one time I was playing catch with this one boy, and this girl came up and wanted to play. We told her no, that it was just a two-person game we were playing. She was mad at us, especially me, I think, and she walked over to Dale and told him that we'd stolen her ball. She'd always lie like that and get the boys in trouble.

"How he punished us was really scary—he'd stick a person in this one room that wasn't being used for anything. It was really dark in there, and really dusty and dirty. There weren't any lights—maybe it was like a big closet or something, I don't know. You'd have to sit there by yourself in the dark, locked up for an hour. It was scary for a kid because you thought there would be spiders or something creepy crawling over you. Your imagination just kind of went wild, you know?"

"IT HAPPENED ONCE IN A WHILE"

Here Nathan stops, clearly uncomfortable. "He would sometimes take off my clothes, too, and kind of touch me. It happened once in a while. It wasn't in that dark room; it was usually in the bathroom, when he'd take the kids in there. I don't know if he did it to anyone else, but he did it to me. I didn't like it, but I was really shy, and I guess I didn't know what I was supposed to say.

"He told me some mean stuff, too. He'd tell me how my parents didn't love me anyway, and how I was a really bad boy, and stuff like that. He told me that my parents didn't mind if he did that stuff to me—that's why they dropped me off at the day care everyday. Anyway, I guess I believed him, because I didn't ever say anything to my parents—not until they asked me about it way later, after we moved away."

Nathan adds that in addition to worrying about his own situation with Dale, he was even more nervous when his little brother began attending the same day care facility.

"It was really separate from the bigger kids' area," he explains, "but it was in the same building. And my brother was still a baby—I worried about bigger kids being rough with him, or maybe Dale or somebody going in there and doing that stuff to him, too. I remember I was always walking away from the playground so I could look at the area where the babies were. I never saw anything, but I guess I kept looking, anyway, just to keep track of him."

Nathan says that he does not remember when his depression started, but his mother has told him about it.

15

"My mom told me that when we moved here from Colorado I was acting real strange, like anxious," he says. "I was five then. She says that I was really frightened and nervous-acting, which I'd never been before. And I was pulling on myself—on my penis," he adds with an embarrassed half-smile, "which is what little boys do when they get real nervous, I guess. I don't remember that part, but I really remember the getting mad.

"But anyway, she was going out to lunch with an old friend of hers named Rene, who was a psychologist who specialized in abused kids. My mom was talking about me and how I was be- having. And Rene said there were certainly lots of things for me to be stressed about—like having just moved, for instance. But she told my mom that another reason for that behavior is sexual abuse, and that my mom and dad ought to talk to me about it.

"So later she asked me about it, if anyone had ever touched me or anything, and I guess I told her yes," he says. "And then later my dad took me aside and asked me the same thing. I told him

Nathan plays basketball with his brothers. Nathan's depression began after he had been sexually abused by a day care worker when he was four years old.

16

yeah, and that it was Dale. My mom told me later that they kind of zeroed in on Dale, since I hadn't really had any close contact with any other people from outside my family. Then I told them I didn't want to talk about it anymore, and I didn't."

"I Wanted to Blame Her"

Because his mother had been advised by Rene to go to counseling if they found any evidence that Nathan had been abused, she called Rene right away. Rene set up a program not only for Nathan, but for his parents, too.

"My parents went to one place where they talked to them about stuff, and I went to a regular doctor, just to have him check me out. Rene told my mom that this was an important part of the healing process, or whatever. It makes kids understand that they are still healthy.

"After doing that for a while, we went for a long time to a place called a rape and crisis center. I talked to people, not always about the abuse—just talked and played."

Nathan does not recall much about the feelings he had then—only that he began having angry moods and explosive temper tantrums that were out of character.

"I yelled and screamed and stuff," he shrugs, as though talking about a different person. "I threw my toys, and I yelled at my mom and dad. I don't think I'd ever acted that way before, really out of control. Mostly to my mom, I guess. I was really mad at her. I sometimes asked her, 'Why did you leave me at that day care?' I was mad at her because I think down deep I was blaming her for all the stuff. It wasn't fair—I know that now, but I wanted to blame her for the bad things that had happened. I guess my parents had known about this from Rene, that it's real common for kids who are abused to snap like that. Once that bad 'secret' is out, the one they were afraid to talk about, kids go from scared to mad."

Nathan gets silent for a moment, then brightens. "I saw this program on these fish called archer fish—they're really amazing. They live in South America, and they eat bugs that live on the leaves of the trees that hang over these little ponds. The reason they call them archer fish is that they spit water out of their mouths, like an arrow, and knock the bugs down into the water where they can eat them. Plus, they're shaped kind of like a bow with an arrow in it, kind of triangular."

ANGER AND SUICIDAL TALK

Trying to drag Nathan back to the subject at hand, the visitor asks if his anger at his mother ever turned inward—towards himself. He nods.

"Yeah, I used to tell my mom and dad that I was going to kill myself. I'd get a sharp knife out of the drawer and walk into the living room where she was. I'd tell her that I wanted to cut myself. She took it away from me and told me that that wasn't good thinking, that I should never talk that way. They loved me, she said, and they'd be so sad if I hurt myself like that.

"I really am not sure if I ever meant it or not," he says, thinking. "I mean, maybe in some way I did. I know one time I went up high on a branch of this tree over our roof. I told them I was going to jump off. They didn't get all crazy and start screaming. They talked to me, calmed me down. My mom says now that they knew that this kind of stuff might happen—I'd talk about killing myself. They learned that in their section of the counseling sessions. But my mom says that even though they knew it could happen, it still made her feel weird hearing me say stuff like that, about killing myself."

Was there medication he could take to help his sadness and anger? Nathan does not think so.

"I'm pretty sure that at first I was just supposed to do therapy and counseling," he says. "I don't remember my mom and dad giving me any pills or anything. Not back then, anyway. But it seemed for a long time that I wasn't getting any better. I'd be better for a while, then something would just get me going again. It was like a roller coaster, my mom told me. I didn't think about it as having to do with depression then—I was too little, and my parents hadn't really talked to me about it. I don't think I even knew the word 'depression' then. Mostly we were just trying to get along, stay kind of happy."

HARD TIMES AT SCHOOL

Going to school was difficult for Nathan, as his parents and counselors had predicted it might be. He was nervous about leaving home and was uneasy at the prospect of a new teacher.

"I'd get real worried at the end of the summer, when I knew I'd have to start a new grade," he says, remembering. "My mom told me later, when I got older, that I maybe was feeling scared because

Nathan's mom attributes his depression and many of his troubles to the abuse Nathan suffered as a child.

of that stuff with Dale. After all, he was a teacher—the first one I ever had. Maybe secretly I was scared I'd get a guy like him again; I don't know.

"I know that almost every year when I was younger—you know how your parents kind of take you in at first and meet the teacher on the first day—well, I was so nervous, I'd walk away from them. They'd be saying hi to some friends they saw, or something—or they'd be talking to the teacher about stuff, maybe talking about me—and they'd turn around and I'd be gone. I'd wander off to another part of the school, or to the bathroom, or something. But eventually, yeah, I'd go back to where I was supposed to be, in my classroom.

"I didn't do so good in school. I didn't have trouble in math, but reading and history and stuff were hard for me. It seemed like I had to take longer than everybody else to get my work done. I wasn't trying to go slow, I just was trying to learn it, you know? Just learn it instead of just reading it fast and answering the questions. So the teachers would get mad because I wasn't getting my work done on time.

"I never acted bad in school, like yelling or having tantrums or anything. But I got sad sometimes. Maybe that made me work slower. But the teachers didn't like me for that, I could tell. I didn't know it back then, but my mom used to talk to the principal or the teacher at the beginning of each school year. She'd tell them that I'd been abused, and I was uneasy sometimes, and for the teachers not to take it personally. She said it was my problem, not theirs, and that if they could be patient, I'd be better off.

"I did have a couple of really good teachers, who my mom says were really understanding about my depression and moods and stuff. One of the teachers, when my mom was telling her about the abuse, understood right away why I ran off the first day. She told my mom, 'Of course Nathan's nervous! Why would he want to trust me yet? I don't blame him.' It turned out that her son had been abused, too, so she knew just the right things to say and do. But most teachers weren't that nice."

"OH, GOSH, I LOVE THOSE GUYS!"

One of the things that keeps him the happiest, says Nathan, is his huge interest in what he calls his "critters."

"I really have fun with them, yeah," he smiles, relieved that the talk of depression and abuse has shifted to something more interesting. "I love all animals, but I really like having the reptiles and amphibians as pets. I don't know exactly why—they're just fascinating, their habits, how they live, how they survive. I like reading about them, too. I just think it's fascinating how they can use their natural defenses—their teeth, their camouflage, their venom, whatever—to stay alive. The idea of survival is really interesting to me.

"I spend like every penny of my allowance and the money I earn paying for either catalogs and magazines, or new pets, or food and supplies for them. I've got a lot of animals, yeah—oh, gosh, I love those guys! I don't have a snake because my mom won't let me. She says when I'm on my own and can live in my own place, I can have all the rattlesnakes and cobras and stuff I want. The only one she might allow is this one called an emerald green tree boa. She says she'd consider that one only because it's pretty and not poisonous.

"My favorites of all my pets right now are my red-eyes—they're real small frogs that live off the coast of Africa in Madagascar. The rain forest, yeah, that's their habitat. So I try to keep their tank nice and warm, and keep a close eye on the humidity. Lots of species are really hard to raise; they're really intolerant if you make the slightest mistake in temperature or humidity—they can get sick and even die. But my red-eyes and my tomato frog are really forgiving. If I goof up a little bit, they can tolerate it, so it makes them easier to care for."

"I Envied the Other Kids"

Nathan says that if he could, he'd concentrate on his pets and forget about school entirely.

"It's a waste of time, usually," he says. "It was hard in elementary school, and when I was like in sixth and seventh grades it got really bad. The schoolwork got harder, for one thing. The teachers got meaner and really blew up if you didn't get your work in on time. I envied the other kids because they got to do fun stuff after school, like play with their friends. But I never could. I had friends, yeah. But every time they'd ask me to do something, I couldn't. I had to work on homework. And that made me really depressed, too. I mean, not just, 'Oh, I have homework again,' but because my work was never over. I hated it because I knew I couldn't ever get it done, and there was no time for me to do anything I liked.

"See, my brothers and me like to do stuff outside. We go looking around in the low areas near our house, where it's really wet. We find turtles, frogs, interesting insects. We usually let those go after a while, but sometimes we keep one. I like doing that, just fooling around on my own or with my brothers."

"Stealing My Life"

"I don't have any friends where we live—my friends were all from school, and we live in a different suburb than my school. It's kind of hard to get together because of that. In our area, the only kid to play with is a ten-year-old. He's okay, but I'd rather be by myself, I think. Usually, I just like to be on my own—fool around with the animals, read, watch television sometimes. I *really* hate school for another reason—it's so early. I'm a night person; I can't get to sleep early. So when morning comes and it's time to get ready for school, I just can't wake up. So that starts the resentment I feel all over again.

"Sometimes I'd just sit there in school feeling like I wasn't even alive, like I couldn't remember how to feel anything. I had no more emotions, not even boredom. It's hard to explain, but it's a little like being yourself and at the same time someone else who is looking at you. When I felt that way, it was like there was nothing in my life that was fun anymore, nothing to look forward to doing. It felt really hopeless, like even my animals weren't interesting. And it made me really mad on the inside, like they were stealing my life away from me, like they were taking every second of time I had. I never got angry, but inside I was thinking how bad that was that they could just steal my life."

MEETING BRUCE

Nathan says that his difficulties with school, as well as the resentment and sadness he felt because of those difficulties, led his parents to seek out a different therapist for him.

"His name is Bruce," says Nathan, "and he's great. I really clicked with him the first time I went to see him. I don't think my mom and dad told me that he was a therapist, they just said he

Nathan and his brothers search through the underbrush for frogs and bugs. Because of his sadness, Nathan went to see a therapist named Bruce. "Me and Bruce . . . played checkers or other board games, and just talked."

was a guy who knew a lot about kids and their problems, and that he might be a good person to talk to.

"I don't know what I was expecting, but he didn't seem like anyone I'd ever talked to before. Even his office was great! There were lots of paintings of wolves and stuff on the walls, and he had lots of Native American sculptures—I liked that. It turned out that he's visited Alaska—that was cool. He raises husky puppies, and we even talked about me getting one sometime and raising it by myself.

"Anyway, me and Bruce didn't sit in a little doctor's office like you see in TV shows about psychiatrists and psychologists; his office was like a living room—lots of soft chairs and places to sit. I didn't have to sit anywhere I didn't want to. We played checkers or other board games, and just talked. He told me about some stuff that he was working out in his life—he says that everyone has things that are hard to deal with, not just kids. It isn't just me, he said.

"He always had hot chocolate there, and that was good. The time always went fast every week when I was there; it was like going over to a friend's house. He told me one thing that was important—he said that if I wanted to do something, I should figure out some way to make it happen. I shouldn't just get mad at my parents or whatever, and blame them for saying no. Bruce says that if you talk to adults in a reasonable way, they are more likely to understand your side of the story, and maybe they'll say yes more often."

Does he still see Bruce on a regular basis? Nathan shakes his head.

"No, things are more hectic now," he says. "I don't see him much any more because everyone is really busy. My parents and my brothers—it seems like everyone is on a schedule, and everybody needs to be driven to practices and games and stuff. I play basketball a lot, and that's fun for me. But I'd like to see Bruce again, stop in and say hello. I feel like he really helped me during the time I spent with him."

HOMESCHOOL

Although Nathan's attitude improved somewhat, he admits that school continued to give him problems. He dreaded going, and he frequently was criticized and berated by his teachers for his inability to get his work done. By the end of seventh grade, he says, his parents had decided to pull him out of public school and teach him at home.

"No, I didn't mind," he says. "I miss my friends at school, but I get to go to this after-school recreation program where I can play basketball and do stuff with other kids. And it's nice working at my own pace at home. My mom is basically in charge. She gets my assignments figured out and makes sure I get work in all the main areas.

"I get to sleep later, too. I stay up late doing homework, or even doing stuff I like, but I know that I'm responsible for getting a certain amount of the work done. My mom works, but I use a lot of the time she's gone to get the homework done. I get to write essays on stuff I care about, like my pets. And after I do the work, my mom goes through it with me and we talk about it. It's not so stressful, and I'm not so sad about things."

A NEW KIND OF THERAPY

In addition to changing the way her son learns, Nathan's mother has also put him in a new kind of therapy called homeopathy.

"It's a way of healing that isn't like regular medicine, like doctors and stuff," he explains. "It's called an alternative medicine because it's based on the idea that your body can learn to fight diseases itself. The diseases can be emotional or physical or mental, it doesn't matter.

"She got into it kind of by accident. See, she's a dental hygienist. She was working in this one dentist's office, but when all the stuff about my abuse and everything came up she quit. She told him she needed more time to spend with me, with getting all the counseling done and stuff. He was really nice about it, I guess.

"Anyway, at a dental convention she was doing a presentation that she put together with a therapist friend. It was about how kids' abuse can have effects many years later in dentists' chairs, or something. And her old dentist was there. He asked about me, and she told him I was having a rough time with depression. He told her about homeopathy, and told her that she might want to look into it as a way of helping me."

Nathan says that his mother pursued homeopathy, reading and studying everything she could find about it.

"She has taken lots of classes in it and really knows what she's doing now," he says. "Sometimes she'll give me a remedy, like a tiny, microscopic amount of the substance that can cause the symptoms in the first place. Like for example, if bee pollen gives some healthy person a bad reaction, a tiny, tiny amount of bee

Nathan concentrates on homework. Rather than attending a public school, Nathan is homeschooled.

pollen in a sick person can cure that kind of reaction. It sounds backwards, but it works.

"So she's been working on stuff that can maybe produce some of my symptoms, like getting sad or frustrated or whatever, and giving it to me in tiny doses. I'm not sure how it works, but I know my moods aren't as bad as they were. And my mom says that even if the homeopathy works for me, there's still a lot of things that I might have to work on, too. Like, for my schoolwork, it's possible that I could have some kind of learning disability or something that makes it hard for me—not just being depressed. My mom had a bad fever while I was born, so she says you never know what kind of things can result. So maybe I'll have to learn some different ways of learning things, or get special help that I haven't gotten before at school, when I go back to regular school."

Will he be going to high school at the public school this fall, or will he be homeschooled another year? Nathan looks worried.

"I don't know," he admits. "I have asked my mom if I could go back to school. She really doesn't think I'm ready yet, but I want to try. I think I could do better. Maybe if I was more upfront with the teachers and told them about things that were hard for me to do, they'd be more willing to give me a break. I mean, that's just what Bruce used to tell me to do—if you want something bad enough, figure out a good way to do it. I hope it works."

ABUSER, PROTECTOR

What about the abuse in his past—has he learned to put that behind him? Nathan thinks a moment before answering.

"I don't ask my mom why she left me at that day care like I used to. I think about it, yeah. I mean, if I'm watching TV and there's something about a little kid getting hurt or abused, I think about it. You can't help it then.

"I don't think I can ever forget about it, but I'm pretty sure that as you get older, it fades a little bit—like it's not so important all the time. But it's not the same as when I was little and thought about it all of the time."

Nathan shifts positions in the chair, sitting up a little straighter.

"I know one thing I wanted to say—one thing that really makes me mad, and you hear it a lot. People use getting abused as an excuse. They use it their whole lives, like because they got beat up or molested or something when they were little, that gives them permission to do it later to other people, even their own kids. I hate that a lot. I remember when this one lady down south drove her car into a lake with her little kids in the back and drowned them. Everybody's saying, 'Oh, she was abused as a child.'

"I don't ever want to think I could do something like that, not ever. My mom says that there's two ways you can be after an experience like mine—you can be an abuser or a protector. I want to be a protector, and I'm sure I will be. I feel protective of helpless animals, or anything being hurt. That was the way I was when I was younger, too. Like I worried about the animals in the pet stores that no one was buying; I worried that no one would ever buy them, and they'd just die in the cages. That would be really wasting a life, just getting no life except being in a cage in a pet store. I'm still the same way, pretty much."

LOOKING AHEAD

Many adolescents who suffer from clinical depression have difficulty looking ahead. They often feel their present situation is bleak, and the future can only be more of the same. But Nathan says that while he used to feel that way sometimes, he is more optimistic now.

"I think my animals have helped me there, too," he says with a smile. "I *do* think ahead, and look forward to new things—I'm always planning something that has to do with my pets. Like I'll be real sad sometimes, just thinking that I don't feel like doing anything, and I'll all of a sudden start thinking about buying a new lizard, or putting in a new cage or something.

"The other day I was thinking how I can make some real money if I could start breeding and selling my red-eyes. People will pay like fifty dollars for babies, and pet shops will give you about half of that. And these little guys have like a hundred babies at a time, so that's good money! I have to get a couple more, though, because right now I only have two males and one female. Probably I'd need two more females and one male to start a breeding colony.

"See, if there are more females, the other females relax more—it's more like being in the wild. There are even tapes you can get of frog calls, so they feel like they have more choices of a mate, like in their natural surroundings. And that seems to produce healthier young—at least that's what most of the magazines I read say."

"SOME OF MY FRIENDS' FATHERS LAUGH AT ME"

Nathan says it is tough finding friends who share his same interests—especially his pets.

"It's easy finding guys who like to play basketball or something," he says with a laugh. "But not too many kids I know like to hear about a species of frog that screams, or a snake with tentacles on its snout. That stuff is the *most* fun for me.

"My mom says that I'm persistent about it, and maybe *too* persistent. Like she says, I'm comfortable only when I'm talking to other people about that stuff, and that I need to learn how to participate in groups. She thinks I need to work on loosening up and talking about other things.

"I don't know, maybe. But it's hard to talk about yourself, about how you feel about things. I think a lot of people have a hard time with that, not just me. She's right in one way, that I have a tendency to hang back when there are lots of other kids. I don't go right in and join. But that's shyness, too. That's the way I am in school, I guess—I just am not a joiner."

Nathan pauses a moment and confides, "Some of my friends' fathers laugh at me. See, I sometimes tell them when I get a new lizard or something. And they'll say, 'Nathan, if you're going to be hanging around with these creatures, how do you ever expect to get a girlfriend?' I don't know about that. They say I'll never get married until I'm forty or something, and even then the woman will be way older than me.

"Maybe that's true; it could be. I mean, I've hardly ever found another *guy* for a friend that likes this stuff as much as I do. There was one guy once, but his big thing was these little red mites. He'd get all worked up if you stepped on one—and they're like as tiny as a flea! I'm not criticizing him, but it was hard to share his interest in them. They weren't anything you could watch very easily, or keep and observe their habits. So that friendship didn't really go anywhere.

"I don't know about the girlfriend part. I'd like to get married someday, and have kids. Maybe by that time I'll make my mom happy and be less persistent, so I can talk about my feelings more, and share other interests."

Nathan holds one of his frogs. More than just his hobby, Nathan's pets are his passion.

He smiles. "But it would be great to meet some girl who loved these critters, too. It would be a great life—maybe before you have kids—to travel around to different places like South America or Africa or Borneo or something, just looking for new species and recording them. I'd like to do that even if I was alone—I'd never miss being around people. But if you had a wife or a girlfriend or something like that, that would be even better."

AN INTERESTING QUESTION

Nathan is convinced that the most exciting thing in the world would be finding a new kind of animal, one that has never been recorded by scientists. Such a find would be rare, he admits, but not impossible.

"It wasn't that long ago that they found some new mammal down in Africa. It was 1990, I think. The animal is like half-zebra, half-giraffe, and they named it an 'okapi.' It's back is like a zebra, with stripes and everything. But the front is kind of brown, with a long neck like a giraffe. And it has some great natural protection, too. If you were to try and pet it, you'd get a lot of black oily stuff on your hand. See, it lives in the rain forest, and the oil keeps its fur from getting molds and other bacteria on it. Nothing can saturate the okapis—nothing!"

Protection and survival seem especially interesting to Nathan. Could that interest stem from the fact that the abuse he suffered as a child was because he was not protected? Nathan looks confused for a moment; then, as he understands the question, he looks interested.

"Boy, I don't know!" he says. "But it's an interesting idea, I don't think I would have thought of it myself. Survival is crucial to any species, and I'm sure animals, including people, who have been hurt are more into survival than those who have it pretty easy. Sometimes I try to imagine what it would be like to be a little tree frog, or a leaf frog, and what it would feel like to be chased by a bigger animal that wanted you for a meal.

"If I were an animal, I think I'd like to be a gecko or something. They can make themselves so hard to see that even experts can be stumped. I read that some scientist had one and invited other scientists he knew to come and see it. Even though it was right on the side of the tank, sitting on a stick or something, none of those guys could find it. Even when the first scientist pointed out the direction it was facing, and where its tail was, the others were still trying to find it."

Nathan often wonders what it would be like to be an animal. "I think I'd like to be a gecko or something. They can make themselves so hard to see that even experts can be stumped."

Nathan says it would be even more fun if he could turn himself into a creature he saw in the movie *Predator*.

"It was the alien," he explains. "When it comes to earth, it uses a special mechanism to actually bend light waves and make itself invisible. If you're looking right at it without knowing it, you would see a kind of shimmery crown around it, like the way the air looks over a hot barbecue or something, kind of blurry.

"Now that would be cool," he says. "I'd love it. I could get on jets whenever I wanted and go anywhere on earth. I could go to some remote jungle and walk up to some snake or insect or something, and just stare at it and study it as long as I felt like. Maybe I'd find one that hadn't been discovered yet."

And what if some other scientist discovered him, with his shimmering crown of light? Nathan laughs.

"I know just what I'd want to be named," he says. "I'd be a *Nathan mysterioso*. That would be just fine with me."

Ryan

"SEE, THE MAIN PART OF THINGS
FOR ME, FOR MY DEPRESSION, IS
THAT I DON'T HAVE NO PARENTS
IN MY LIFE. I GOT NOBODY THAT
LOVES ME."

*Author's Note: My first thoughts on hearing Ryan's story were, "How
could anyone who has lived this life not be depressed?" His has been a
"throwaway" life, rejected by one parent, abused, and finally rejected, by
the other. The system has had difficulty with Ryan, too—being unable to
help him express his anger nor move on.*

*In his backpack he carries pages of notes from his counselor at his last
group home. The counselor mentions bipolar disorder as well as clinical
depression as Ryan's problems, although Ryan's admitted substance abuse
is not mentioned. Ryan mentioned several times in the course of our interviews that he has been given prescriptions for medications, but because
of the recreational drugs and alcohol he uses, he has been unwilling to
take them. No one has tried to help Ryan with his drug problem so that
he can be treated for the mood disorders which plague him.*

Ryan is a little overweight, and younger than he sounded on the telephone the night before. He called after seeing the sign downtown—
someone interested in talking to kids suffering from depression.

"I don't know what you mean," he had said when he called.
"But I'm real sad all the time, and I have papers where the coun-
selors told me my problems were caused by depression. Anyway,
I think about killing myself a lot."

Today, standing shivering outside the library in a thin blue
jacket, he seems far younger than fourteen. His black hair is

slicked back and he is smoking a cigarette, but those things only make him look more like a little boy trying to act older. He is lugging an old gray backpack and looks as though he has been on the road for months.

FEELING HOLLOW INSIDE

Ryan lives on the streets, but plans to move with relatives to Utah—almost one thousand miles away—as soon as he can get enough money for bus fare. He is what many child protection workers call a "throwaway"—a child who is on his own because his parents don't want him.

"I've stayed at my mom's a couple of days," he says with a friendly smile. "But she doesn't want me around no more. She told me I could stay two days, tops—then I'm supposed to be out. I can't stay in no homeless shelters because I'm fourteen, and I'm not with no parent. But I'm sort of hanging around with my aunt and uncle, and they're going to let me come to Utah with them on the bus.

"I know they got places for runaway kids to go, but I've gotten kicked out of most of them. Fighting, usually—or doing drugs. I was in a group home until a few days ago, but I ran away from there—didn't want to be there at all. So I'm kind of out of luck right now. The bad thing is that I'm under age, and I look young. That means I get stopped more by cops than older teenagers do. Anyway, I went from the group home to where my mom works downtown; I asked her if I could please stay and live with her a while, since I'm out of luck. But she just gave me five dollars, and told me to go somewhere and get a hamburger. She said she'd think about it."

Ryan says the attitude of his mother makes him feel hollow inside.

"It's a feeling I'm used to feeling," he shrugs. "I got this thing called clinical depression, and it's like the way you feel most of the time. But yeah, when my mom says something like that, I feel real bad. I don't know if she realizes it when she's handing me money instead of letting me stay, but it's a big deal to me. You get all achy inside, just like you got the flu or something."

"IT'S JUST EASY TO BE PESSIMISTIC"

Ryan will be fifteen next fall, but he has not gone further in school than eighth grade.

"I didn't go at all this year," he says. "I don't like it at all. When I do go, I've gone to special schools for people with disabilities or behavior problems. I've kind of got both, I guess—I've got depression. I've always known it, even before I got diagnosed last year.

"See, I get sad about everything; I can't really react any way except sad. I don't feel happy because I don't allow myself to, even when something good happens. Like today, when this one lady at an adult homeless shelter said she'd pay me five dollars if I cleaned all the tables in the dining room and did a good job at it, but what I do is figure I'll do a bad job, or she won't like me, and then the job will end. You know? It's just easy to be pessimistic."

Ryan says he gets discouraged and sad over things just like other people, but that it's not really the same feeling.

"If you get yelled at by your dad, or you got dumped by your girlfriend—I consider those *little* things, man. I mean, it's not a big deal at all. You feel bad for a couple of hours, but then you're back on your feet again. With me, I stay depressed for too long. This one counselor told me that I react inappropriately. He's the one who tested me, looked me up and down like a regular doctor, and then told me about taking some drugs to help my moods.

"Maybe it sounds like I'm just a baby, like I'm feeling sorry for myself, but that's not it. If you were me, you'd know—I mean, you just can't help it. It's like I have no control over what I feel like. If I thought I had one more cigarette in my backpack, but I really didn't, that's like no big deal, right? But some days, I get as sad about that as you might feel if your parents died. That's what I mean, it's just something you can't change."

"I SHED ALL MY TEARS WHEN I WAS YOUNG"

Sometimes Ryan's sadness turns to fatigue and he can't seem to get enough sleep.

"I sleep for like eighteen hours at a time, then I wake up and all I want to do is go back to bed," he says. "And other times, if I'm tired and I can't sleep—like if I'm on the streets or something and can't find a bed—I'll get really mad inside. Like once I was talking to this teacher at my old school, and she said something that really made me feel bad, and instead of getting depressed, I started punching holes in the wall with my fist! No kidding, I broke a clock and made like four holes in her wall.

Ryan sits on a street corner. "I stay depressed too long," he says. "This one counselor told me that I react inappropriately."

"One time a social worker told me that maybe I should cry more often, let that sadness out. She said it would be a release for me, so I don't keep everything inside. But my dad says that I shed all my tears when I was young, so I don't have no more now—that's why I can't cry. I don't know. Like I said before, my counselor at this group home I was in thought that my mood swings can be controlled pretty easy if I was on some medication, but I can't take that stuff. See, I use other drugs like hash, speed, stuff like that. And I know I'd screw myself up more with the medication."

Ryan pulls on his lower lip, lost in thought. "You know," he says, "I never thought about this before, but my mom makes more than enough money to let me stay with her. She's a head janitor at this big office building downtown, and she's making nineteen dollars an hour."

He looks apologetic. "I shouldn't keep talking about this, but that kind of thing makes me realize that my life has been pretty f—— over. Sorry, but that's like the only way I could describe it, I guess. If I told you about what's been happening to me in the last fourteen years, maybe you'd understand."

AN UNWELCOME BABY

He was born in the city, he explains, to a mother who didn't want him once she was told her baby was a boy.

"She only wanted girls," he says without much emotion. "She already had a one-year-old daughter, and she didn't want nothing to do with no boys—I mean, she's told me that since. My dad moved away to New York like two weeks after I was born. They weren't ever married, so there was no divorce or nothing.

"So she put me up for adoption, and when I was six months old, a family took me. I don't remember much about them, except that their house was right by a park. I used to play on swings there, I think. But that's about it for memories. When I was almost four, my dad came back from New York and decided he wanted me. Since he was my biological father or whatever, he got custody since all the legal stuff for the adoption hadn't gone through.

"I don't really know why he wanted to get custody of me. I mean, he must have, since he took that family to court over me. He told them he never gave up his rights as a father, and so he was contesting the adoption. He got his way and everything, and he took me.

"It sounds kind of nice, but now I look back and I say, boy, what a stupid move on his part. He just f—— me over, too, because why did he come all that way just to get me when he didn't even want me? But that's getting ahead, I guess."

MOVING TO NEW YORK

Ryan says he vaguely remembers going to court with his father and his adoptive family.

"I remember this old black judge who didn't like the fact that my mom had given me up for adoption," he says. "I mean, she didn't have a job, but geez, she was making like six hundred dollars a month on welfare. That was more than enough to support me. Plus, my mom lived like two blocks from a food shelf [food bank], so we could have gotten help when we needed it.

"Anyway, the part I remember was that the judge thought my mother had been ridiculous to give me up for such a stupid reason—that she didn't want a boy. So he tells my dad, fine, if you want to take care of your son, then do it. So my dad took me back with him to New York, like the very next day."

Ryan says that his dad did not fit anyone's stereotype of a father.

"He's a biker," he says with a smile. "He really was. He cooked really good, too. One time he and a friend of his opened a restaurant on the third floor of a library in the town where we lived. He worked during the day, and I stayed with his wanna-be wife"—at this Ryan snorts derisively—"or sometimes at the neighbors, until I was old enough to go to preschool.

"I remember upstate New York as a pretty happy time, at least for the most part. There was lots of space there to ride a bike, or play around in the woods. I remember playing on a big mountain of snow that collapsed on me, and I got frostbite on my face. But that was the only bad thing when I was little."

"MY PARENTS CALLED ME 'BABY SMACK'"

Ryan says that his parents were both drug users—before he was born, and afterwards.

"My dad wasn't doing drugs so much when we were in upstate New York," he says. "I mean, he was, but not as bad as he has been other times in his life. He was mainly into pot, acid, 'shrooms— same junk I'm into now. Not really serious stuff, I don't think. He was pretty mellow, pretty easy to get along with then.

"My mom—I don't really know what she's doing now, but back when I was little, my parents called me 'Baby Smack' because when my mom was eight months pregnant with me she was still shooting up heroin. I told my counselor about all this stuff, and she says that there's no way of knowing if all them drugs has something to do with my depression now. I mean, that could have something to do with why I get so sad, and so mad.

"I don't really know," he says, shrugging his shoulders. "It might be just an excuse. I did start doing drugs myself when I was sort of young—about seven. I smoked my first two joints with my dad when we were fishing one time. So maybe it wasn't completely my parents' fault. But really, they were both heavy into it.

"My mom, she used a lot of crack when I used to stay with her back a couple of years ago, after my dad kicked me out," says Ryan. "It affects her, yeah. I mean, you always know when she's using. She used to lock me and my sister in the bedroom while she

Ryan speaks with a homeless man. Ryan spends most of his time on the streets since both of his parents seem uninterested in helping him.

had some guy come in with a needle in his arm, and she wouldn't let us out of there. My sister really freaked out—she thought my mom would forget about us, and she was scared that that man would kill her."

Asked whether his father knew Ryan had smoked marijuana in his presence when he was so young, Ryan laughs. "Yeah, he knew. He was the one who showed me how to roll a joint in the first place—he told me to go ahead. I wasn't doing nothing behind his back!"

"MAYBE I'M JUST TOO STUPID TO LEARN"

After a couple of years, Ryan's father decided to take his son back to the Midwest, although Ryan is still unclear why.

"I'm not sure about the details," he says slowly. "I know that where we moved was near where my grandparents lived, so maybe that was why. I don't think the reason was money because I remember he always said the restaurant was doing real well. But anyway, we moved, and that was sort of the beginning of the bad stuff for me.

"I never really fit in anywhere after we moved. I hung out a lot by myself mostly. I didn't like school that much because I was bad in it. Up till second grade I wasn't real terrible, but after that I had lots of trouble. See, I can't spell. I read excellent, but can't spell. Even my little sister is way smarter than me. I can't even do my times tables, and I know that's being pretty stupid. I decided after a while that the school can't teach me anything. I mean, maybe it's not the school's fault, maybe I'm just too stupid to learn. But they weren't teaching me, so why should I go? I mean, not every kid is a brain. I don't even feel like trying hard when all it gets me is bad grades—and then I just feel sad all over again."

Besides his trouble in school, Ryan began getting into trouble for shoplifting in his neighborhood.

"Getting in trouble was what I did mainly," he says, with a self-mocking expression on his face. "I've heard that mainly from my dad. According to him, my getting in trouble was what screwed up his whole life, so he can't live normally like any other man. Ask anyone in my family, they'll tell you I'm a screwup.

"What I did was steal. Like once I stole $135 worth of jewelry from the Kmart. I got arrested for it, right at my own house. That was bad for the neighborhood's reputation or something, so the landlord kicked us out of the place we were living. That happened other times, too—my dad was really mad. Why did I take the stuff? I'm a thief, I guess."

"HE JUST TOLD ME I WAS A LOSER"

The Kmart incident was his first arrest, but Ryan admits there were plenty of others. Unlike a lot of teens who shoplift, he says, he was not motivated by peer pressure.

"Most of the stuff I do, I do by myself. Like I told you, I was usually by myself. I'm by myself almost all the time, and I like it fine. I don't feel funny being alone. Plus, there's less chance of somebody else cracking under pressure if a store detective or somebody comes up. I can handle my own situations. And if I can't, I can always run—without worrying if someone is keeping up with me.

"Anyway, my dad whipped my ass that first time and grounded me for a month. I'm sure he was mad at me, but I'm also pretty sure that he didn't really care that much, either. We never really talked about it—he didn't ask me why I did it or anything. He just told me I was a loser, and no good, and that that stuff was pretty much what he expected out of me. It was a mistake for him to ever come back to get custody of me. He told me that all the time."

Sometimes Ryan stole bikes, or even cars, and he was often successful at it.

"The best money I made was grand theft auto," he says, with more than a hint of pride in his voice. "You just ride around in the car for a while, and then sell it for parts if you can find a pond. That's a chop shop, or whatever, where you can sell the vehicle for parts. There's lots of them around the city, and lots of people can tell you where."

A Lifetime of Drugs

Whenever he was caught, his father moved—either because they were told to by landlords, or because his father wanted to avoid confrontations with children's services workers.

"I know he was using drugs," says Ryan. "I mean, I'm sure now, looking back, that he was probably just as scared about himself

Ryan sits with his sister, who lives with their mother. Ryan claims he "didn't like school that much because I was bad in it. . . . See, I can't spell. I read excellent, but can't spell. Even my little sister is way smarter than me."

getting into trouble if the police came around as anything else. But I believed him then, when he told me our bad life was because of me.

"My own drug use then was getting worse. I mean, those joints at seven weren't the end of anything! In fact, I didn't even get high that time, I remember. I tried it again the very next day, and I got high for sure then. When I was doing the stealing, that was pretty much what I used the money for.

"I'd drink, too. I remember one friend I had—Jesse—he lived near me one time. He looks like me, only he has blond hair, but everything else is the same. He's been doing drugs since he was in kindergarten. And it was Jesse's grandpa that got us going on the drinking part—that guy used to give us both shots of whiskey to share when we were four!"

Ryan knows that his drug and alcohol use are not helping him; however, he says that the highs he gets sometimes help him forget his depression.

"I know maybe the pot and the other stuff isn't great for me, but I don't want to give it up. Not now, anyway. I sometimes go overboard, I know that. I mean, I got arrested for public intoxication one time—I drank a whole bottle of tequila by myself and passed out on a bench by the downtown library. I went to detox; that was when I was twelve, I think. You sure don't want to get caught doing stuff like that because then you're all in the system, have to talk to cops and social workers and stuff. But I drink to get away from feeling sad, and I drink when I'm happy, too, because I know that soon I'm going to feel sad. I just got to be careful and not overdo it.

"But the stuff's so easy to get—it's like going to get aspirin or something. It's always out there. I mean, I've been able to score hash and acid and stuff since I was eleven. I knew a guy who used to sell to my cousin, and then I just got his pager number and started calling him on my own. I never had any trouble getting stuff after that."

ABUSE IN HIS FATHER'S HOUSE

As Ryan got older, his father became increasingly angry at him, and often the anger turned to violence.

"He hit me a lot," says Ryan frankly. "A pretty abusive family all around, mine was. I mean, even the times when we came back here, and my mom would have me—like when I was twelve or thirteen—there was abuse. My dad was the worst, though. He put my face through a window once, and I had to go to the hospital to get stitches. After that I got so mad I went outside and just punched a tree as hard as I could. I broke my knuckles, and I had to have more stuff done at the hospital.

"One time I got so mad putting up with the abuse that I took a knife and almost went after him with it. I took a pocketknife out of my pocket. He backed away from me; he was only as far from me as you are now. Just a few feet. I was going to throw it, but at the last minute I threw the knife at his foot. As much as I hated him, I just couldn't stab him. He's my father, after all. But you know what? He called me a loser then, too—for not stabbing him with that knife! Anyway, he was drunk at the time, like he was lots of other times when stuff like this happened. I think the time he put my face through the window he was mad because he thought I'd taken one of his cigarettes.

"I had lots of scars and stitches. There was always some mark from a punch or something. And yeah, family services came out and asked some questions, but nothing ever came of it. The time he pushed me through the window, the child protection workers came so late that the cuts on my face had almost healed."

"I DON'T WANT TO SEE HIM"

Ryan's depression has been a major factor in his life, he says, since he was twelve or thirteen. That is when his father became more involved in drugs, and also more abusive to Ryan.

"I got diagnosed with all this stuff when I was back at my mom's for a while," he explains. "See, the Christmas before last I got in a big fight with my dad. I stole something from one of his friends."

Ryan looks uncomfortable, as though he does not want to go into much detail about the theft.

"It was drugs, yeah," he says, finally. "He was a dealer, this guy, and I was going to take a little of what was in his bag. I figured he wouldn't notice a little missing, but I was wrong. My dad and the guy weighed the bag and found out there was an ounce missing. And my dad came at me, really drunk and high, and started beating me up, like a fistfight. I fought back, too. It ended up that he hit me with a hose, and I picked up a saw and hit him with that. I left, he left, and I haven't seen him since; truly, I've never set eyes on him since that Christmas.

"I've talked to him a couple of times on the phone—really short conversations, with me doing none of the talking. But I don't want to see him. I hope I never do, I swear to God. He says his whole f——-up life is completely my fault, and if weren't for me he'd be having a great time. I hate him, but that's okay with me. I know he feels exactly the same about me."

Ryan's eyes begin watering a little, and his voice has become choked.

"My counselor says I have to be mature enough to look beyond my dad's words, since my dad isn't that mature. I have to know that he was f—— up before I was even around, and he's just using me as a scapegoat. But I don't feel like cutting him breaks. I don't feel like being mature enough to ignore his words. You know, that shit hurts."

Ryan is crying now; he rummages through his backpack and comes up with a dirty shirt, which he uses to wipe his eyes.

"I don't want to talk about him no more," he says.

"I Don't Have No Parents in My Life"

Ryan sniffs a few times and folds the shirt back into his backpack.

"I should be used to this stuff, only I'm not. See, the main part of things for me, for my depression, is that I don't have no parents in my life. I got nobody that loves me. Nobody wants to take care of me. It's not like I need a lot of taking care of, but you know what I mean. I feel like I'm the only person in the world who feels that way, too. So my counselor says that's why I get depressed so easily; and that's why nothing ever gets better, since nothing ever changes between my parents and me, and it ain't going to, man. My clinical depression is partly environmental, my counselor says. That's stuff that won't change until my situation changes, like where I live, and who with.

"After me and my dad had that fight, I wasn't living with no-body. I was sleeping on the streets because I couldn't go back to him or to my mom. Neither one wanted me. My mom had me for a little while a couple years ago, but she threw me out because she still doesn't like me. She doesn't do well with boys, she says, and she gets real mad because I fight with my little sister."

Has he ever tried to talk to his mother, to explain that it really hurts his feelings when she throws him out?

"Yeah, I've tried," he says. "She just says she doesn't want the responsibility, and she don't care if that hurts my feelings because it's the truth. She's twenty-nine, and says she's been taking care of herself all her life, and she does okay. My mom always says the same things my dad says—'You're big enough to take care of your-

Ryan's drug use prevented him from finding a place to sleep in youth shelters. "I just found places to crash, and that was the only tricky part. Sometimes it was hard finding places to sleep that the cops wouldn't kick you out of, or arrest you."

self. You're fourteen, act like it.' They say my uncle was taking care of himself since he was thirteen, so I shouldn't be crying about having nobody taking care of me."

GROWING WEARY OF LIFE ON THE STREETS

When Ryan first became homeless, he was able to stay in youth shelters. However, either because of his drug use or his anger, he was no longer welcome at those places and had to find shelter elsewhere.

"I just found places to crash," he says, "and that was the only tricky part. Sometimes it was hard finding places to sleep that the cops wouldn't kick you out of, or arrest you. For a while I'd go late at night into this one motel and sleep on the stairways at the end of the hall. There's a door, and people can't really see you until they are leaving and walking downstairs. By two o'clock in the morning, though, there aren't too many people coming and going, so I can stay warm and hidden. But the concrete stairs aren't comfortable, and you never really sleep, you know? I got caught there a couple of times, though, so I don't trust it anymore. Mostly I stay awake at night, just walking and hanging out at all-night places, and then taking naps during the day in the library. I just pretend I'm reading, rest my chin on my hands, and sleep.

"If I got bored, I'd steal a car and go riding around for a while. Not to sell it or take it to a pond—just to ride around. I'd bring the car back later, not too far from where it was parked before. I just need to move around when I get real bored or tired, and the car helped.

"I carried a gun back then, and that was because I was selling some crack," he admits. "That was how I earned money. I don't have the gun no more, though, because it started scaring me. I'd think about it, like how I could use it to kill somebody for no reason. Or I'd start thinking about killing myself when I got depressed. You know,

Ryan walks the streets. "Mostly I stay awake at night," he explains, "just walking and hanging out at all-night places and then taking naps during the day in the library."

sometimes it just seems like the best thing would be to put my head down and go to sleep and never wake up. Everything is just so much work. And when I'm not feeling that way, I'm in a rage about something else. I once threw some matches in the gas tank of a car, just because I was mad at my father—and he hadn't even hit me that day!"

SOCIAL WORKERS AND COUNSELORS

Because he was tired of living on the streets, and because his depression was frightening him, Ryan called his social worker and asked if he could be placed somewhere that he could get some help.

"I got placed in a facility up north, a place for kids with problems," he says. "I didn't do much of what they wanted me to do. I'm not sure why. I didn't go to classes, didn't work out a schedule for myself like I was supposed to. I mostly got in fights with other kids, and got evaluated by the psychologists there.

"That's when I found out what was wrong with me—at least the main thing," he smiles. "It was depression, the clinical kind. I found out that thoughts about killing myself were common among kids with depression, and that lots of kids suffered from it. That's also when I found out about the medications they can give you for it. Aside from the medications the psychologist offered, all he did was write up a twenty-page paper which basically said I had a raw deal in life. But aside from taking medication, I guess there was nothing I could do about it.

"But like I said before, I was straight with the counselor and told him about the other drugs I use. He said no, don't mix those drugs, that could be dangerous. He told me I got to make a choice; but right now, I'm choosing the fun drugs. I'm not ready to stop those yet. Depression's bad, but having no weed to smoke, or acid, or whatever—no, I'm not ready for that yet."

Ryan says that he also learned that social workers cannot always be trusted.

"The one lady up north was a liar," he says flatly. "She wasn't supposed to talk about what her and I talked about to other people, but she did. She talked to my dad—I know that. I guess he never denied the stuff I told her, like him beating me up, and taking drugs, and stuff like that. I mean, he knows he did all that stuff, so what's the use of lying? It's not like he was worried about the courts taking me from his home. I was already out, and that's what he wanted—he just didn't want me put *back* into his home!

But it still really pissed me off that she wouldn't hold things in confidentiality, like she promised she was going to do."

WHAT I WANT

Ryan's fantasies used to get him through his early bouts with depression. He would daydream about things he would do someday, things that he could look forward to in the future. Now, however, Ryan has grown too cynical to believe the future offers hope.

"I want to have a job and a place to live," he says simply. "That's my life goal. I know it doesn't sound like much, like some kids want to grow up to be better than Michael Jordan, or richer than a king or something. But I don't have goals like that because that's all bull unless you got parents. I can't see nothing really great in the future, I just don't see it happening. I'll be really happy for that bed, I'm telling you.

"Money's short right now, so there's day-to-day things to worry about. I got eleven dollars now. I smoked a joint with my aunt a little while ago, and used some money for that. I haven't been selling no drugs for a while because I don't want to be doing it without a gun. I could sell a little bud [pot], but there isn't much money in that for all the time you spend on the streets, and there's the risk. So I've been working cleaning tables, like I said."

What about his personal life? Does he have a girlfriend? Has his horrible family experience soured him on the idea of a family someday?

"Maybe I'd have kids someday, maybe not," he says, looking indifferent. "I have a girlfriend, yeah. It's my aunt's cousin, but it's not incest because my aunt and I aren't related by blood. We have sex, yeah. I use condoms, so I ain't worried about having kids any time soon! I don't see getting married or anything. How can people do that now—there's no money for lots of people.

"I mean, look at my aunt and uncle, the ones I'm going to Utah with. Tomorrow morning she's going over to the Kmart parking lot, a few blocks from my mother's house, and she's going to panhandle. She's done it before. But how can you buy things for a family when you got to do that? It's crazy, I think.

"Lots of times now I'll be walking inside some store, just to stay warm, and I see TVs on. They have on shows about families, or commercials about cars or driers or something. Everybody, man—they look so happy. And I feel worse because I never will be like that. My counselor told me that it's all bull on television, that people aren't

Ryan hopes to move to Utah with his aunt and uncle (center). "I'm hoping that in Utah I can stop taking drugs.... I'd like to solve this depression and stop having these feelings all the time."

like that. I want to believe him, but I think part of the television stuff is true; and then I feel like I'm really missing out. It's hard to explain. I'd like to go fishing with my dad, if he were a different person."

FOR RIGHT NOW

Ryan's goal now is to raise $86; then he will be allowed to make the trip to Utah with his aunt and uncle.

"I'm not sure what they're going to do out there," he says. "But they say that the life out there in Utah is lots cheaper. And the Mormons who live there, they'll treat you nice. They believe in sharing with people, even if you don't have the same religion as them. So that sounds pretty good to us.

"I'm hoping that in Utah I can stop taking drugs. Maybe there won't be enough of them out there, and I'll have to stop. I mean, maybe there aren't as many dealers. I could maybe get medicine then and start getting well. I'd like to solve this depression and stop having these feelings all the time."

What would he tell other kids his age about feeling depressed? Ryan rolls his eyes.

"Wow, I'm the very last person who should be giving anybody advice about anything. I mean, I'm a screwup, and I don't even handle my own stuff right. I feel half the time like hurting myself, and half the time like hurting other people. *That* sure isn't good advice. I don't take my own advice, let alone other people's. I just hope people aren't stupid like me and take the bad kind of drugs so much they can't take the drugs that will help them get well.

"I know there are three things that make me start getting depressed—they're almost guaranteed to get me in that bad mood where I feel sad and angry. One is when people tell me I'm not worth anything. And when people don't care about me—people who should. And the last is when they are telling me what I should do, or how I'm living my life all wrong. I say, hey, you spent my whole childhood showing me they didn't want to be part of my life, and now when I try to do things on my own, they're in my face telling me I'm wrong all the time. Screw them, I say."

"One Big Joke on Me"

Ryan says that hurting himself has been easy. Several weeks ago, he says, he attempted suicide.

"I cut my wrists with a razor blade," he says. "I was in the garage at this one guy's house when I made the cuts. I was thinking, 'Boy, I'm going to really die; I'm finally getting out of here.' I wasn't really sad or scared. I just thought about how there better be some better place, like heaven, or the whole thing is one big joke on me.

"Then some guys came in with a blunt [a marijuana cigar] and they saw me bleeding. They asked me what I was doing, and then I told them to get out, that I was fine. But they didn't believe me and ran off to call the cops. An ambulance came and took me to the hospital. I was on forty-eight-hour suicide watch. Then they let me go. I'm telling the truth, see?"

He pulls up the sleeve of his sweatshirt and reveals an ugly, jagged scar on his left wrist.

"I sometimes think about what my mom and dad always said— like how I'm no good, I'm a loser, I'm a screwup. Maybe that's right and this whole thing is my fault. Then I play this game where I'm allowed to take one thing back that I did, and I figure out if it would change things. One of my things to take back was going fishing with my dad and having him show me how to roll joints. But the best one I thought of was just being born. That's the only one that would solve everything."

Runa

"I JUST FELT AS THOUGH I'D
ALWAYS BEEN SAD, AND SAD WAS
THE WAY I WOULD ALWAYS BE."

Author's Note: I met Runa after putting up a notice about clinically depressed teens at a youth center in the city. Like Ryan, she has had a terrible childhood. However, unlike Ryan, she has pursued counseling and therapy to rid her of her problems, and has tried various medications to help her bipolar disorder.

Runa's therapists have suggested to her that even though her childhood was very troubled and very abusive, it is not the cause of her disorder, only one of the factors that has triggered it. It is no use, she mentioned more than once, to whimper about other people (specifically her mother and grandfather) ruining her life. It is not self-pity which motivates her, but the need to move on, to put the past behind her in some meaningful way. She has attempted suicide in the last year, but seems now to be more in control of her own life. She appears to me something of a success story; although she is still working through her problems, she is also busy creating a path for herself—a path that includes college, a job, and supportive friends.

Runa—an alternate spelling of "Rene"—opens the door to her apartment. She lives in an old brownstone, and her apartment is tiny but immaculate. The oak floors gleam; the walls are decorated with prints and photographs. She does not have many visitors, she says, so she throws a couple of pillows on the floor in the living room for her guests.

Runa is of mixed race—an attractive combination of Native American, white, and African-American. Patches of her short black hair stick out from under a baseball cap worn backwards. Her smile is easy and genuine. Runa's face is not the image of a depressed teenager.

"I'm really glad to hear you say that," she says with a grin. "My appearance hasn't been like that all of my life. In fact, if you had seen me walking down the street a year ago, I would have looked a whole lot different. My head was always down, I walked all hunched over, and I couldn't meet anyone's eyes. I didn't want to attract anybody's attention—I just wanted to be invisible. I'm not saying I'm in great shape now, but I'm getting better, I think."

"I CAN'T REMEMBER EVER *NOT* BEING DEPRESSED"

Runa says that she was diagnosed by a psychiatrist as suffering from clinical depression just a few years ago, but adds that she knew all her life that something was wrong with her.

"I'll tell you—you can't spend as much time as I did sleeping, crying, just thinking about being dead, without realizing that that's not normal behavior," she says. "In fact, I can't remember ever *not* being depressed. I believed that most of my problem was environmental—that is, it was triggered by stuff going on in my life—but there was more to it than that. There was just something— I don't know—kind of strange about the way I thought, the way my thoughts jumped around.

"Now I'm able to look at my life in a more detached way. See, I don't live with my mother anymore, and that was the main cause of my problem. And I don't want to sound like I'm blaming other people for my problems because I know now that she herself was crazy—psychotic would be a better word. But truthfully, I had a horrific childhood. I can't think of a way to say it that doesn't sound overly dramatic, but there it is. It was a nightmare."

Runa takes a deep breath to calm herself. "I'm from here, from the city. I lived in the projects with my mother. I don't have any memories of my dad. They'd split up a long time ago. I knew he had sent me a game called Connect Four or something like that, and that it was my favorite thing to play when I was little. And I had a mustard seed necklace from him, too. But that's all."

"YOU HAD TO KNOW HER TO UNDERSTAND"

She says she can remember asking her mother what her father was like, what his name was, but she got vague answers.

Although recovering from her depression, Runa says "you can't spend as much time as I did sleeping, crying, just thinking about being dead, without realizing that that's not normal behavior."

"She never said his name or anything good about him," Runa says. "But once in a while she'd drop some bombshell on me about my father. She'd be flipping through a magazine at the kitchen table and would come to a picture of Sylvester Stallone, and she'd say, 'You want to know about your father? Well, that's him, right there.' She told me that she'd been artificially inseminated with his sperm by some doctor back in 1976. She said the doctor did it right here, in the kitchen."

Runa laughs grimly. "I know this is really odd-sounding. She was just so strange, though, so odd. It's hard to describe without sounding like I'm making this all up. You had to know her to understand. But anyway, she'd say something like that about Sylvester Stallone, and then another time she broke down crying and told me that she had a friend named Thomas who agreed to sign my birth certificate. That was another story. Why couldn't she ever be straight with me? I don't know."

Runa says that a few years ago, after she left home, her mother had to have a psychological evaluation by the county to determine whether she could regain custody of her daughter.

"That was one of the many times I realized she didn't care much about me," she says quietly. "It took her more than nine months to get around to making the appointment—nine months! I never heard the official results directly because by that time I'd given up on her. I figured that she was in no hurry to have me back, so how much could she care about me?

"But my own therapist told me later that my mother was basically an undiagnosed schizophrenic, or else had multiple personalities. Either way, she was really out there, you know? Both of those possibilities made a lot of sense to me. You know, I have no idea where my mom's problems began, or anything like that. I have a full-time job just dealing with my own. Through therapy, writing in my journal, just thinking, I'm getting some of it sorted out."

A Breach of Trust

"Probably the beginning of all my problems happened because I was sexually abused by my grandfather when I was very young," says Runa. "I was five when it started and eight when it stopped. Too little to understand about what my grandfather was really doing, only that I didn't feel good when it was happening. He used to call it our 'nap.'

"The first time it happened I was lying on top of my grandfather on the sofa at my grandparents' house. My mom and I sometimes went over there to visit—my grandfather would come over to our building and pick us up and bring us back to his house. I know I told my mom afterwards about his touching me, and that it made me feel afraid.

"In fact," she says thoughtfully, "that was probably one of my first memories of my mom just going off. We were at my grandparents' kitchen table, and she was screaming at my grandfather, telling him he had no right to do that to me. She was really letting him have it. He wasn't saying much back to her, I remember that. And I remember my grandmother scoffing at the whole thing, saying that I was a silly child and was obviously lying to get attention."

The abuse continued, says Runa, even though her mother had seemed so angry at her grandfather. "It's like she got mad once and then just let it go," she says, shaking her head. "Maybe she just didn't know it was going on, but I doubt it. I *do* know that my grandmother was very aware of the abuse, even though she had denied it that first time."

"Hey, Grandma, Why Don't You Say Something?"

"I can remember her actually being in the room while it was going on. She had some of those long whisker hairs, you know, like some older women have? Anyway, it was when we were taking one of those 'naps,' and she was in the room standing by the mirror, plucking out those hairs. My grandfather had put this oversized quilt over the two of us, you know, and he was molesting me. She kept looking over and then looking away. I was thinking, 'Hey, Grandma, why don't you say something?'"

The sexual abuse continued for nearly four years, until she was almost nine years old. By that time, it was a constant occurrence and had intensified. And because none of the adults around her were concerned, says Runa, she says she was confused as to what to do.

"I was scared sometimes, but sometimes the feeling was pleasurable, and that was confusing," she says. "And I was going to school in third grade and learning about 'good touch–bad touch.' It's almost funny in a sad way! I wanted to yell out to the teacher, 'Yeah, I know what that bad touch is! Hey, you want to meet my grandfather?'

"Years later, when I was in a group home after I'd gotten away from my mother, there was this one girl my age who had been molested, too. She was so helpless, though—we had to take turns escorting her to different rooms that reminded her of places where she'd been molested. I wanted to tell her, 'Deal with it!' I wanted to tell the people at that group home, 'If I had to be escorted everywhere that reminds me of where my grandfather molested me, you all would have to be walking around with me twenty-four hours a day, every step!' Bathroom, bedroom, garage, coatroom, kitchen, living room. I mean, come on!"

Runa smiles sheepishly. "I guess you could say that I don't like to be a victim. I feel like some stuff happened to me that I couldn't help. I don't want to be a prisoner of that, be afraid all the time. I get angry with people who use it as an excuse to just fold up and refuse to go on."

How It Feels to Be Depressed

The abuse stopped, she says, when she was almost nine. Her mother had seen it going on, and later that night yelled at her.

"She told me that if I ever so much as walked into the same room as him, she'd kill me," says Runa. "She was so mad I figured she wasn't exaggerating. I was upset that she felt it was all my fault, but in a way I was glad that I could finally be free of him. I had an excuse to stay away from him, and I did."

If she thought her life would be better after that, Runa says, she was really mistaken.

"All I did was think about it," she admits. "I don't remember obsessing like that while it was going on—maybe I did, but I don't know. But afterwards, instead of feeling glad, I felt really empty, really alone. I didn't even feel angry; that might have been healthier for me. But I just felt alone and very, very tired.

"Now, of course, I know that's what real depression feels like. But to someone who has never felt it, it's almost impossible to explain. I cried all the time. I was tired; God, I was so tired it was hard to hold my head up. The more I slept, the more exhausted I felt. I didn't want to think because even thinking was too much work."

Runa shrugs, impatient with her lack of appropriate words. "It's like I was in this big jungle, and no one could hear me. I wasn't even sure I could hear myself. But I kept crying just to hear something that was real, just to remind myself that I existed, so I wouldn't just get swallowed up by the jungle."

As a child Runa was sexually abused by her grandfather. She says, "I just felt alone and very, very tired."

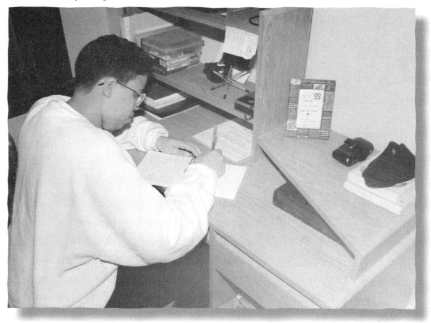

She laughs. "I think I'd have been better off not trying to explain it—it sounds *really* strange now. But the thing I want to stress is that no matter how hard it is to believe, I wasn't able to think logically—like, this is the reason I'm sad, and if I do this, this, and this I will eventually feel better. I just felt as though I'd always been sad, and sad was the way I would always be."

"She Got So Crazy"

Runa says that as she sunk into the depths of depression, her mother seemed to be getting more psychotic, her behavior more unpredictable and strange.

"She hit me a lot, punched me, slapped me," remembers Runa. "She got so crazy, I thought she wanted to kill me. Nothing I did was ever right. If I was in another room doing something, she'd be screaming at me that all I did was ignore her. And if I sat in the room with her to keep her company, she'd stop talking, get up, and leave the room. If I was doing my homework, she'd accuse me of not listening to her. If I ate something and she hadn't made it for me, she'd get mad. And if I tried to do something nice for her. . . ." Her voice trails off. "Ah! What's the use? It never stopped."

Runa admits that she loved going to school back then, just to get away from her mother.

"She didn't have a job; she'd been on welfare since before I was born," she explains. "She was hardly ever gone, so when I was home it was just the two of us—and I hated it! I wanted to leave for school early, just for the pure and simple reason there were sane people there. It would have been easier at home, I think, if there'd been a bunch of other kids so she'd have to divide up her craziness among all of us, but no luck there. Just me. She'd roam around all night, going from room to room, talking to herself, talking to the radio. It was just crazy."

Anger and Sadness

It was during junior high school that Runa began feeling rage as well as sadness and depression. In the past she had considered running away, but her cat Coonie kept her from going.

"We had seven or eight cats back then," she says. "But my mother hated Coonie. I really thought that if I left, she'd have done something horrible. And most of the time, I felt like the only two friends I had in the world were my stuffed bear and Coonie.

"But even that changed. Instead of being loyal to Coonie, I wanted to hurt him. I remember picking him up one time and throwing him all the way across the room. He was so surprised—I guess he'd never thought I would hurt him. But I did. God, poor Coonie—he never did anything wrong. The only thing he did was have the bad luck to live with my mom and me, the craziest house in the world. I still feel so bad about that. I mean, I didn't kill him or anything, but just for a moment I wanted to."

Besides taking out her anger on her cat, Runa began to hurt herself. "I know now it was attention-seeking stuff, back in junior high," she explains. "But I'd cut myself, hit myself against corners and tables until I was black and blue. My wrists, especially, would be just blue from bruises. I'd spend my lunch hours running around a nearby lake so I could mess with the barbed wire around the golf course down there.

"I'd use rocks, razors, knives, whatever was handy. And then I'd rub lotion on the cuts, really make them look red and sore—and it hurt like hell, let me tell you! Like I said, I wanted people to notice me, to feel sorry for me—I'm not really sure. Instead, I should have been talking to people and telling them what was going on, just going up to them and saying, 'Look, this stuff is going on in my life, and I need some help here.' But I couldn't do that. I couldn't get the words out very well then, and I still have trouble now."

Did it work? Did she get the attention she was seeking? She smiles. "Yeah, oh yeah. I'm sure my friends all thought I was nuts. They told the teachers; they tried to talk to me, but I clammed up. It got to where only occasionally would a teacher take me aside and ask me about things, but most of the time nobody would."

NO SLEEP

By the time she was in high school, Runa knew her life was in shambles. Her mother's abuse and erratic, strange behavior was frightening, and Runa herself was wavering between severe depression and rage.

"I think of my life when I was fourteen, fifteen years old as something out of the movie *Whatever Happened to Baby Jane?* Did you see that one? I mean, two people just doing crazy things to each other, just out of control. I remember sometimes being so sure she was going to kill me that I would have plans for each room, where I would run to get away. What could I pick up to defend myself? What could I use to kill her first? 'Kill her!' I mean, I'm actually thinking those words! I knew down deep that there would be a time when I would be forced to kill her, just so she wouldn't kill me. All I needed was a plan, I kept thinking."

Runa says that when she was in high school, her mother began waking her up at night for no reason.

"It was sleep deprivation at its worst," she says with a sad smile. "I mean, scientists have shown that rats go crazy when they aren't allowed to rest, and I'm sure that's what was happening to me, too. She'd come in to my room at like three A.M. and wake me up out of a deep sleep. She'd say, 'Where's that thing?' And I'd say, 'What thing, what are you talking about?' And she'd get mad, telling me not to take that tone with her. And she'd say, 'Where's that bag that your friend gave you a Christmas present in two years ago?' And I'm like, 'What? What are you talking about?'

"It was so bizarre, so strange. But she seemed really serious about it. Nothing she said, though, made any sense. Why was she prowling around at three o'clock in the morning? I have no idea. And when I couldn't answer her questions, she'd get crazier and hit me. You know, I used to say, 'I love you, Mom,' to her at night before I went to bed, hoping that would buy me some grace, so she wouldn't wake me up. But she would anyway, almost always. It was like she knew how desperately I needed to sleep, but she was determined that I wouldn't."

TAKING CHARGE

When she was fifteen, Runa decided that she needed therapy. She knew she would get no support from her mother, so she took matters into her own hands.

"I went to my eye doctor—I had an appointment to get my glasses prescription rechecked," she explains. "And while I was there, I said to him that I wanted to start therapy and asked him how I should do it. He and the nurse helped me find the numbers in my insurance book, and I started calling numbers right from their office. It took a while, too—you know how insurance companies keep telling you to talk to so-and-so, and you keep getting transferred.

"So eventually I was connected with a therapist who set up an appointment for me, and I went. You *bet* I went!" she laughs. "And it worked out so great, too. I mean, it was a perfect time. You know how sometimes you feel bad and you wait and wait for an appointment for the doctor, and then you finally get in and whatever it was doesn't hurt anymore? Well not this time! I was feeling so bad, so small and unimportant. Between my depression and my mom, I felt like I was the most useless, ugly, stupid thing on the face of the earth. I deserved to die, that was what I felt like.

"I got along great with the therapist—she was really intelligent, and a good listener. So we got started on a regular therapy schedule, and it felt so good to be getting some of this out, you know?"

No Help from Child Protection

It was not long, however, before her mother found out where she was going and began sabotaging Runa's relationship with her therapist.

"She started canceling my appointments," Runa explains. "She'd call in and say I couldn't make it because I was sick or whatever. The reason is because she was certain that these appointments wouldn't be covered under her welfare plan. But that was the great part—welfare *did* cover this, I checked. But she refused to believe that it wouldn't cost her something, and she decided to put an end to these appointments."

Runa says that it was her therapist that caught on to her mother's plan.

"My therapist got mad at my mom," she says. "She told her that she was aware that I was dangerous to myself, very suicidal, and that if my mother didn't allow me to keep my appointments, she would call child protection to have me taken from the home, so I could receive help. This was during my wrist-cutting stage," Runa adds.

"And the next day in school, child protection shows up and the workers sit down with me. I show them my wrists, but because they were self-inflicted, they couldn't prove that my mom had driven me to do it."

She sighs, and shakes her head in disgust. "You know, all these agencies say they are there to serve the kids, to represent them. But really, everyone is so worried about the parents' rights, the parents getting mad, they end up not believing the kids. I told the truth to those child protection people, but they did nothing. So I don't give them much credit. You hear all the time about some kid getting murdered by their parents, and then when they look at the records, wow, what do you know? Child Protection had been called and they did nothing."

GETTING OUT OF THE HOUSE

Runa was introduced into the juvenile justice system during her first year of high school. She had planned to go shopping with a friend one evening, she says, but her mother refused to allow her to leave the house.

"She started yelling at me to come inside, but I told her no," Runa says. "I knew there was no reason at all for her to refuse to let me go— I'd done my work, done my homework. She just didn't want me to leave.

"So she told me I'd be sorry if I didn't obey her, and she took her cigarette and burned the inside of my arm. I don't know if she meant to do that or if it just happened. But she knew she'd done it, and she threw down the cigarette real fast and rubbed it out with her shoe. Anyway, she told me again that if I left, I couldn't come back. She slammed the door and locked it. So, I guess the decision had been made—so I went with my friend."

Runa says that she was only temporarily happy to be out of the house, for she knew that when the evening was over she had nowhere to go.

"I had an aunt, and there was always my grandmother and grandfather's house. But no way was I going there—I didn't ever want to see my grandparents again," she says. "And I knew my aunt wouldn't understand any of this—my mother had refused to talk about what my grandfather had done to me to anyone. No one would believe anything. And I could have spent a night or two my friend, but I would have had to answer a lot of questions, which I didn't want to do.

"So I turned myself in to a juvenile center," she says with a smile. "I spent the night in a holding cell there, and it was all right with me. And one thing was good—the officer that was on duty there was the same guy who was the liaison officer at my high school, so I knew him. That helped me, anyway.

"They had a social worker for me the next morning, and once again," she says with more than a trace of bitterness, "the system was unable to help me. I had the burn mark, but no proof. Hey, I could have produced my friend as a witness—she saw the whole thing—but not good enough. I think I pretty much had to be dead before anything would be done.

"What they *did* do was leave a message for my mom and told her where I was. And you know what? She waited for three whole days before she called. Three days! Boy, that alone should have clued those people in on how great a relationship my mom and I had. When she did call, she yelled at me, told me she hadn't called earlier because she hadn't felt like walking the three whole blocks to a pay phone. I'm in a detention center, and she's worried about a little walk to use a phone!"

Runa was released to her mother's custody, a fact which she says was very confusing to her. "I asked my social worker, 'What are you going to do about this? All she's going to do is yell at me about some pointless thing that has nothing to do with why I'm here—like doing the dishes or something.' And I tell the social worker about the times she wakes me up in the middle of the night and how I'm starting to go crazy like my mom.

Although Runa's mother was very erratic, Runa still thinks of her. "You know what the hardest part of that whole time was? It was realizing that my mother didn't even miss me."

"But the social worker didn't get it. She's like, 'I have no control over what chores your mother wants you to do—that's her right as your mother.' I couldn't make her understand that it wasn't about doing dishes; it was about waking me up at three A.M. and about beating me up, about being crazy and talking about crazy things."

Runa's voice had gotten loud as she recounted the scene with her social worker, but she quickly lowered it to almost a whisper.

"You know what the hardest part of that whole time was? It was realizing that my mother didn't even miss me. That sounds nuts, even to me, but even as bad or crazy as she was, I wanted her to want me. Just because I was her daughter, and because I had no one else. But she didn't want me. She hated me. And it just got worse when we got home."

"It Was Sleep Deprivation"

Runa stands up and stretches, moves around the little living room. "I think of this time as almost like being a POW [prisoner of war]," she says. "It was sleep deprivation—way worse than ever before. It was as though she knew about how lack of sleep makes you crack up, and she was bound and determined that she was going to do that to me.

"One of the things she would do was come upstairs—again in the middle of the night—and flick on the light switch, then off, then on, just click, click, until I woke up. I was groggy and stood up and turned off the bright light. She said, 'I wouldn't do that again if I were you.' And she went downstairs. And then she came back up and turned the light on again—click. And when I turned over to get out of bed to turn it off, she was standing there with the biggest, thickest walking cane I'd ever seen—solid wood. She held it over my head, like a weapon. I'll just say that I believed that she was going to beat me with it; and as a result, I learned real fast how to sleep with the bright light on.

"There was another thing she did that freaked me out, too. She would come into my room quietly in the middle of winter and open my window. Then she'd turn on the fan. It was really cold— we're talking about below zero here—and she'd sit in the chair right next to me and wait until I woke up. I asked her why she was doing this—I was so cold I was crying—but she wouldn't let me close the window or unplug the fan. She said, 'I want to give you pneumonia like you gave me.' I'd never had pneumonia, hadn't ever given it to her, but again, there was no reasoning with her."

Such battles with her mother were draining her of all energy, she says. Her depression was becoming worse, and the beatings were getting more severe.

"Every time she said something to me, it was about how stupid and worthless I was, how no one could care about me because I was useless. Then she'd dump out my hamper of dirty clothes and start whipping me with a dirty pair of blue jeans. She was a big woman, probably two hundred pounds, and when she put all her strength in those blue jeans, that really hurt.

"It made me afraid while it was happening, but after it was done I felt relief and then just depression. It was a cycle, like a regular routine. I wanted to die, I wanted her to die. I didn't know exactly what I wanted, really. I'd be with other kids sometimes, but I didn't feel like I fit in, like there was this voice in my head that put me apart from everyone else. I couldn't talk much to them, and so there were automatic limits to those friendships. I knew I was different, that when I went home to my apartment in the projects and my mother, that we ceased to have anything in common, me and those friends. And then I'd go talk to a therapist or social worker, and they'd tell me to try to forget about it for a while and enjoy being with friends. I just didn't fit."

"GET ON THAT BUS"

Runa had always liked school, both for the time it gave her away from home, and because she was a good student. Her regret, she says, was that she could not stay at school longer each afternoon.

"My one dream was to be able to join the tennis team," she remembers. "I was pretty good at it, too. But my mother wouldn't let me stay after for any reason. I had to take the first bus home every day or there'd be hell to pay. I didn't want to run the risk of getting her angrier than she already was.

"But one day I had to stay. I had been sick one day and had missed an important chemistry test. If I didn't take it, I'd get a failing grade, and no way was I going to let that happen. So I called her from school, begged her to let me stay after, just once. I offered to put my teacher on the line so that she could hear for herself that I wasn't lying.

"But no, she went off on me like always, calling me a bitch and telling me what a liar I was. She said, 'Get on that bus or you'll be in terrible trouble.' I hung up the phone and walked real, real slowly toward the buses. There was my bus in the line—I could

Runa helps out at a youth center for teens who have experienced some of the same things she has in her life.

have caught it if I ran. But it was like my feet refused; I wouldn't run. I watched the bus pull out and knew right away she was going to beat me when I got home. I could visualize the whole thing."

HELP, AT LAST

So, says Runa, she found her counselor and told her what had happened. She explained that she had missed the bus and that her mother would maybe kill her—literally—or, at the very least, give her another severe beating.

"It was so funny how it worked that time," she smiles. "I stood there in the counselor's office and listened while she called the district supervisor, who told her to call 9-1-1. Well, she did, and the police came! And because I'd been in therapy, and I'd been under suicide watch at the juvenile center, they took me seriously this time. I don't know, really, what changed—why they believed me this time. But I was just glad they believed me!

"I was taken by the authorities to a children's shelter, where I would be safe from my mother for a time. Then later I was transferred to a home for girls. Boy, I remember walking in that home—I was like yes! I'm home! A month later I had a hearing, and then a month after that a pretrial, and then I was taken into a foster home with some really nice people who actually cared about me. My mom lost her custodial rights over me forever. I could have stayed there in the foster home until I was eighteen, except things hadn't completely turned around for me."

TERRIBLE THOUGHTS

Runa says that the trouble was her own doing—she just could not handle the peacefulness of her new home.

"I know it sounds odd," she shrugs, "but it was way too calm. I'd never lived with calm before, and that was hard for me, I guess. I started getting in lots of fights with my foster mother's daughter. I had lots of anger, and I let it all out. I know I created a lot of scenes that really belonged back in my mother's house, not there in foster care. In therapy afterwards, we talked about the idea that maybe since my mother wasn't around anymore for me to react to, I had to invent trouble.

"Whatever it was, it frightened me really bad. See, before when I expressed anger, it was toward myself. I'd feel stupid and ugly and worthless, and I'd think about being dead or about hurting my cat or banging up my wrists. But all of a sudden, in foster care I was having these really gross thoughts, scary thoughts I'd never had before.

"The first time I noticed it, I was fighting with the foster mother's daughter, and her father was there in the kitchen. I remember looking at her father, and all of a sudden I started visualizing him as a fish, and me with a knife, and I was slicing him, gutting him." She shudders involuntarily. "It was so spooky because it was as if I could actually feel that I wanted to do that, to kill him that way.

"Or it would happen in the store where I had a part-time job. I'd visualize the craziest scenes, like killing the customers with hammers and then trashing the store and setting it on fire. These were more than thoughts, they were like—like very realistic daydreams. It scared the hell out of me, honestly."

CHECKING IN

Runa was so unnerved by her realistic, violent fantasies that she hurried to a hospital and asked for help. She was fearful, she says, that if she did not get help soon she might actually hurt someone.

"I called my foster mom from the waiting room," Runa remembers. "I asked her to meet me there, if she would. When I think back at how I behaved in their house, I wouldn't really have been surprised if she hadn't shown up. But soon afterwards, there she was, in the middle of the night, hugging me.

"We went to the crisis department and talked to some people there. I explained to them, you know, I've been suicidal before and have thought hard about killing myself, but now it's about other people, and I was really scared. They sent me to another psychiatric facility that would help me, with doctors that specialized in helping people with problems like mine.

"The very next day I was diagnosed. I had what's called 'bipolar disorder.' What it meant was that I was having these really drastic mood swings, back and forth between huge, scary highs, where I was having my fish-gutting fantasies, to low, low depressions, where I just wanted to curl up and die. Sometimes when I'd go back and forth between highs and lows, I'd just black out, not remembering what I'd said or done. Sometimes I'd feel like I was hallucinating, too. I'd be talking to my therapist and I'd look down at my arm or something, and it would be my mother's arm! It completely freaked me out."

"Medications Have a Bad Side, Too"

Runa says that a great deal of her stay in the hospital was spent talking with psychiatrists and therapists.

"We talked about my life at home with my mother, and the stuff with my grandfather. A lot of my problems, they said, were environmental and would get better the longer I was removed from my violent home life; but it would take a long time, and some of the behavior would need to be controlled by medication.

"I think people should realize, though, that just getting on some pills isn't like this complete happy ending. It isn't like when you have strep throat or something and you get penicillin and you're okay in a couple of days. See, medications have a bad side, too—especially when they are strong chemicals to control your behavior. I had a lot of trouble finding the right medicine. The side effects of these things were unreal.

"Don't believe me? Hey, the first medication I was on, the doctors were sure it would help me right away, that I'd notice a big difference. I did, all right—I started gaining weight, really getting heavy. See, the pills were made from some salt, which makes your body retain water, that's why. To make things worse, I was always thirsty. And the worst part of all is that I lost control of my bladder—I started wetting the bed at night."

She sighs. "See, since I'd been abused as a little girl, I'd had that bed-wetting problem before—that's a major aftereffect of sexual abuse. The bed-wetting had been an embarrassment back when I was nine and ten—but at sixteen—man, it just wasn't hitting it, you know? I couldn't sleep through the night, and even when I did manage to wake up in time, I couldn't always wake up soon enough—you know what I mean?"

Runa says that the doctors did not want to lessen the dosage of the medication for fear that it would not help her mood swings. Instead, they continued to experiment with different medications, hoping the pills would help her without giving her unpleasant side effects.

"I tried another medicine that gave me huge hives, and then another that made the hives even bigger," Runa smiles. "We were running out of drugs to try, and I was thinking that I'd really like to get better without being medicated so much, you know?"

A BAD TIME LAST SUMMER

Runa says that since that time she has really tried to cut down on the number of medications she takes, hoping she can rely on herself to get well. It has been two years, and she has seen improvement. However, it has been a grueling process—one that has its frightening moments.

"Last summer I had worked myself down to just one medication, and that wasn't too bad. But even though I was usually okay, I had a major relapse. I somehow got it into my mind that I was going to kill myself on a Friday. I was living alone—not with my foster family anymore, since I was eighteen. But I didn't feel unhappy—that was why the suicide idea seemed so strange. I had a job, had some friends that I enjoy being with.

"It was like I wanted to get a sign or something from God that I shouldn't go through with it. It was like I was daring myself. So on this one Thursday I had the time of my life with my friends, going to the amusement park, going out to eat, and even having a big sleepover with my friends. But the next day, I went home—that was Friday. One of my friends called me, and I'm thinking does she hear in my voice that I'm thinking about killing myself? But no, she just acted normally, like nothing was different."

Runa takes another deep breath and continues. "So I felt like I was fooling everybody—that I could feel so bad, so sad, and no one even knew. So I decided to dare myself, or God, or whatever—tranquilize myself and see if I wake up. If I did, I'd never do anything like that again. If I didn't, well. . . .

"I shut off the fan, turned off the radio, turned off my answering machine, just downed hundreds and hundreds of my pills. I am serious, I took like nine hundred pills of one type, and hundreds of others. They were so nasty, like horse pills. And I lay there, felt bad, and then fell asleep.

"About four hours later I woke up, sick as a dog. I was throwing up and had diarrhea, all at once. I was sitting in the bathroom with the garbage pail in front of me, just wishing I had died. I didn't call anyone; my heart was palpitating, beating so fast you couldn't believe it."

"SO WHAT ARE YOU GOING TO DO NOW?"

Runa says it felt so strange to go to work the next day as if nothing had happened. She told people that she had overdosed the night before.

Runa looks through college course catalogs. She is most proud of applying to college and hopes to attend a liberal arts school.

"One of my friends looked at me and said, 'Okay, Runa, so what are you going to do now?' I'll always remember that—it was kind of like the most important question I had ever been asked. Now that I had that behind me, what *was* I going to do?

"With my therapist, I worked out a kind of plan. We talked it over and decided that from then on I was going to start talking to people, really communicating with them about my feelings. And I wanted to be off *all* medication, not just *most* of it. I knew in my heart I could do it, and at the same time, I knew it would be hard. But I was determined to work hard at being free of all of the chemicals, all of the reactions to the medications. I don't like putting my life, my personality in the hands of doctors."

She laughs. "Hey, it's a practical solution, too. I was paying sixty-five dollars every three weeks for that stuff, and to get a refill I had to take a bus ride out to the suburbs where my psychiatrist has her office. The ride was long—transfers and everything made it like an hour. Plus the wait in the office and the thirty-minute appointment, then home again. It was expensive and time-consuming. I pay rent here, and it's expensive, even though my place is small. I don't need the stress of earning money to support my 'drug' habit."

"I'll Always Be Fighting the Battle"

Runa says it would be nice to say she was completely cured, but she knows better.

"It's a little like being a recovering alcoholic," she explains. "I'll probably always have the impulse to be back and forth with my moods, but I can work on controlling it. I can beat it back to the point where the symptoms aren't evident to other people. But I'll always be fighting the battle—that's what I'm setting my sights on.

"Do I have ways of coping now? Absolutely. I force myself to talk to my friends, which wasn't always easy. I do things to relax, like write in my journal."

She leans back and takes a children's coloring book from the bookshelf. "And see, I color. This is like the most calming thing in the world. It's something I can concentrate on, but it's easy. I can be a kid—my therapist says that in some ways I've never been able to be a kid. I don't get embarrassed at all; I buy new coloring books all the time!"

Runa says she has also learned to take stock of the things that she worries about. "I have always tended to make mountains out

Runa finds coloring to be therapeutic. "This is like the most calming thing in the world. It's something I can concentrate on, but it's easy."

of molehills. I used to go to work and be all hyper and rant and rave—all because I forgot to mail in my phone bill or something. Now I try to think about keeping stuff in perspective. That way I can control my moods, not be depressed and cry all the time.

"And yes, sometimes I still do. I cry and worry, but then I pick myself up and make sure I call somebody that will understand, get out of the house, talk to my bear, whatever. I'm busy lots of evenings helping as a volunteer at youth groups or taking part in support groups for people with my condition."

She walks over to the telephone stand by the door, where three thick paper booklets are stacked.

"I'm proudest of this," she says, grinning. "I'm applying to three liberal arts colleges. I want to go this fall. I'm hoping for Beloit in Illinois. I'm going there in a couple of weeks to see about scholarships and look around. I'm meeting with the admissions director. I always want to feel like there's something just around the corner, something to look forward to. College would be the absolute best!"

Julia

"I THOUGHT I WAS SO DIFFERENT FROM EVERYONE ELSE. THERE WAS A LITTLE PART OF ME SOMETIMES THAT WANTED TO BE THE SAME."

Author's Note: Of the four interviewed for this book, Julia stands as the classic "clinically depressed" teen—a young person whose depression seems to have had no environmental or chemical triggers. Although she has had difficulty with the police (an assault felony charge) and is currently homeless, Julia's depression began as a child. She speaks very matter-of-factly about being sad as a small child and not being able to verbalize why. Even today, she is not sure of the cause, only that she "wanted to be isolated." When her concerned mother tried to understand the source of her little girl's sadness, Julia says that she had no explanation other than "Mama, I'm just crying. Just crying."

Her family did not seek help for Julia. It was not until she was "in the system" after her arrest that she was diagnosed as clinically depressed. Her therapist gave her Prozac, but she says the medication did nothing for her, only make her more angry that people were telling her what to do. Today she is still off medication, but angry and impatient with almost everyone with whom she comes into contact.

Julia stands outside the door of the homeless shelter, trying to pry a wad of blue bubble gum off the sole of her sandal with a twig. She is here in the homeless shelter—temporarily, she hopes—until she and her infant are able to move into an apartment. Julia is seventeen, a new mother, and a chronic sufferer of depression.

"I Am Just Answering Questions to Be Polite"

"Yeah, I am a depressed person," she says with a blank expression. "It's not that I hate talking about that, it's just that I hate talking, period. I'll be honest with you, I am just answering questions to be polite. I'm not trying to be hostile, it's just I hate talking.

"I'm not from here originally, no. My family moved here from the west side of Chicago back when I was eight years old. I had just started school that year—it was in September—and we kids moved here. See, my mom and dad weren't getting along too good, and so my mom took us kids and moved up here. My grandma and granddad were already here, so it made it nice to have relatives."

Julia's family is a big one, she says, and her mother worried about her children adjusting to the move.

"There are lots of us," she says. "I have a twin brother, Julius, and then I have other sisters and brothers. It was four of us kids at first that came, and two weeks later my older brother and sister came, too. Eventually, my dad came up here to live, too, but he and my mom didn't get along. Later on, when I started being sad more and more, my mom used to ask me if I missed Chicago," she remembers. "I don't think I did—I don't know what I would have missed. We lived in the projects there, and it wasn't that nice. I didn't really have no friends, so that wasn't it. So I don't think the move was a big thing one way or the other."

"It Started Probably When I Was Born or Something"

Julia cannot recall the exact time in her life when her depression began; nor can she remember a time when she was not depressed.

"No, I don't want to say *depressed*, you know, like people say they're depressed because of something or other. Like you're depressed because you hate the way your hair looks, or you are depressed because you had a fight with your mother. That's not what I mean. It's a whole different thing with me.

"See, I have always felt that I didn't like being around other people. Maybe at first my family thought it was shyness, you know, how little kids are like bashful? But it wasn't that way with me. I wasn't bashful, I just didn't want to have people around. In Chicago I'd sit out on the steps away from my brothers and sisters

Julia claims that she wants to be isolated: "I have always felt that I didn't like being around other people."

and any of the other kids. I just wanted to be by myself. It was all the time, and it started probably when I was born or something."

Asked to elaborate on those feelings, Julia just shakes her head.

"I know you don't get it—nobody does," she says. "See, I wanted to be isolated. My mom and dad didn't understand either. In fact, when I got a little older, my mom talked to me about it. She said that's all I've ever been is alone, and when I was really little, she remembers me always crying about something. And maybe then she thought I was wet, or hungry, or whatever. It's just when she started laying it all out—all the years—that she saw that it was just *me*—the way I am."

Julia remembers talking to her mother about the crying. She told her that it was not about being sad, or having hurt feelings, or not having a sucker when all the other kids have one.

"I said, 'Mama, I'm just crying. Just crying.'"

NO HELP FROM JULIUS

Julia's brother, she remembers, was especially concerned about her.

"Being a twin, we were always kind of aware of each other's pain," she explains. "We don't look alike, or anything—we're just

72

like all the other sets of twins in my family, one short and dark-skinned and one tall and light-skinned. But we think the same about each other. We're kind of tuned in. When one is in trouble, the other one is right there.

"But even with Julius, I didn't know what to say to him. In fact, we ended up fighting. He was trying to be close to me, hugging me and trying to make me smile. But I kept telling him I didn't want to smile. I would push him away and hit him, and he'd get mad back at me. And that made me feel even worse. It just kept going like that with Julius. He still is that way, as a matter of fact. He knows that of all of the children in the family, he is the closest to me. And if I would talk to anyone it would be him. But I usually don't say nothing to Julius."

Julia says that her desire to seek isolation did not arise from any cause that she knew of—that is what made it so difficult to verbalize when she was young.

"I know my mom loved me because she was trying all the time to solve me, like I'm a puzzle," she says with a frown. "She didn't get mad at me like the rest of my family, just concerned. I think her feelings were hurt, too. I just kept telling her, 'Nothing,' when she asked me what was wrong. I didn't know no words to explain it better."

FROM SAD TO MAD

Julia says that her unwillingness to talk seemed to create unpleasant situations, even in school.

"It was like all of a sudden no one had anything else on their minds to think about except making me smile or making me talk. I wasn't doing it for no attention, that's not it. I was just tired of people, didn't like them. And then all of a sudden I'd get real mad at them. School was a good example. I hated school, hated sitting in those desks next to other kids. I hated the idea of eating in school, too. I'd *never* eat anything in school; that was disgusting to me! Teachers would try to get me to eat, but I wouldn't. Sometimes I would make up lies about having a stomachache so I could go home. It worked for a while, then they stopped letting me go home. I would get mad at them if they talked to me, too.

"One time, back in Chicago in first grade, this teacher was trying to get me to color on this paper bag with a monster outlined on it. I didn't want to do that. She just kept telling me how much fun it would be, and I could choose the color I wanted for the monster. I just sat there, looking down. She just kept on jabbering about it, and I got mad. I picked up a crayon and started just scribbling on the bag, really messy. Well, she got so mad that she sent me out in the hall and yelled at me. I started to cry, and I'd never, ever talk to her again, not even a word. I hated people who did that to me!"

"Maybe a Fire, but I Don't Know"

As she got a little older, Julia says her bouts with depression became even worse.

"I would just start getting sad," she explains, scowling. "Like, I'd be sitting there thinking about something, just the littlest thing, and all of a sudden I would just feel so bad. It wasn't about anything big, just way out of proportion. Like, I'd think, man, I wish my walls in this room weren't so dirty. And then I'd get so sad, like someone died or something! And that thought, that one sad thought, would make me stay in my room, so I couldn't do nothing about it.

Julia tends to her small baby. Before the birth of her daughter, Julia says she "wouldn't eat, wouldn't shower, wouldn't wash my hair, wouldn't do nothing but sleep, or sometimes cry and sleep."

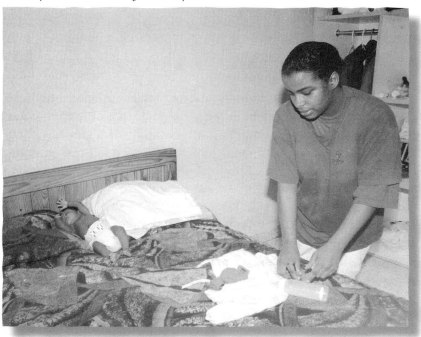

"It was like I was paralyzed or something. I'd be lying on my bed and my legs wouldn't get up, even though I thought I should maybe do that. And I'd just lie there. I wouldn't eat, wouldn't shower, wouldn't wash my hair, wouldn't do nothing but sleep, or sometimes cry and sleep. I'd sleep sometimes for days in a row, just waking up once in a while and going back to sleep. I wouldn't even get up to go to the bathroom—in fact, one time I got really constipated from my body just shutting down. I ended up having to go to the hospital and having lots of enemas and stuff.

"Nothing was important enough for me to get up for, really. Not for a party, not even if it was my birthday. I don't like Christmas, don't like Easter, either. One time on the Fourth of July, I remember my mother cutting up watermelon for all the kids outside, like a picnic. They was all scrambling around, getting their pieces. But I didn't care, I just sat there like a dead person or something."

Could she think of anything that would have been important enough to make her leave her room?

"I don't think so," she says thoughtfully. "The building being on fire? Maybe a fire, but I don't know. I don't really think so, not when I was like that. It would be days before I'd come out of my room."

NOT A NORMAL TEENAGE GIRL

So much talking and explaining has frustrated Julia, and it is clear from her body language that she is winding down. Her shoulders slump, and she talks with a sigh in her voice.

"When I became a teenager, I wondered about myself. I thought I was so different from everyone else. There was a little part of me sometimes that wanted to be the same. I used to imagine what it would feel like to go to the mall to shop, or going to movies with friends, like a normal girl. I'd wonder about going on a date and getting ready for it. I used to have these other thoughts, you know, really strange thoughts, and I'd think, 'Do other people think about stuff like this?' Like I'd try to imagine what it felt like to shoot yourself in the head, whether you would feel it or you'd die first. Or I'd wonder if you jumped out a window, would you die of fright while you was falling, or whether you'd just smash up on the street, and what that felt like."

She smiles faintly. "I know that all sounds really morbid. But see, that's what I mean, I thought about that stuff, even when I was young. Then I'd think, man, I'm not normal at all! That's not the kind of stuff other kids my age think about.

"But that was only once in a while. Mostly, I didn't care whether I was different or not. That usually didn't matter to me. I know I'm saying it over and over," Julia says, shrugging, "but I hated the whole idea. I didn't want to see any of those people, I didn't like the noise of all those voices talking about stupid things. I don't even like grocery shopping!"

Julia gets up and stretches. She says she is tired—too much time up during the night with her baby, who was fussy. She has grown tired of the talk, and she would prefer to be upstairs in her room at the shelter.

DROPPING OUT AFTER SEVENTH GRADE

It is a sunny morning, three days later. Julia seems almost disappointed that her visitors have arrived. She is tired, her eyes half-open. She gives a resigned, bored sigh and sits down.

"I had other problems in school I forgot to tell about," she begins. "See, I have this dyslexia or whatever you call it, too. It means I get the order of letters or numbers all wrong sometimes. That makes it hard to do math or read or anything like that. So I had trouble in school doing the work.

"Lots of times I skipped school because I didn't want to go and just sit there. If I'd have gone and knew what was going on, I'd probably have gone even though I didn't like anybody talking to me. But feeling stupid and not talking—that wasn't worth it, I thought. Plus, those teachers were mean; they didn't like me at all. So I'd leave. No, my mother didn't know what was going on, she thought I was there at school all the time.

"I'd get in trouble sometimes; the truancy officers would call at the house. But usually I was fine. Lots of times I'd go over to my aunt's house; she didn't care what was going on at all. I'd just hang around there all day."

"I PICKED OUT LIKE THE FIRST ONE I SAW"

By the time she was in eighth grade, Julia says, she had had enough of school. She stayed home most of the time, although occasionally she tried a new way out of her depression—boys.

"I'm not saying I liked boys, 'cause I didn't. And I don't now, either," she adds quickly. "But I had this cousin who was always telling me I was stupid to just sit around not doing anything. She'd say that it was real nice to have a boyfriend, that it could change your life a lot. So I tried it.

"I had a boyfriend—I picked out like the first one I saw. He was a friend of my brother's, I think. I was with him a year and a half. I hated him, too."

But why go through the pretense of having a relationship with a boy that she hated? Julia has heard the question before and nods.

"I know it's stupid. I just felt sorry for him, I guess. He wasn't bad or anything, it's just that I hated talking to him, hated being around him. I just thought it might make me feel better, having someone like that. But it didn't. I don't care about any of that, one way or the other. I hate sex, too—that was a big disappointment. I found that out when I was thirteen and tried it. I don't want to share myself with anybody else, not my feelings or my body. I just don't like being close to anyone. I like to keep myself away from the other person's words and feelings—then I'm safer. Like I said, I

Julia at the laundromat. She claims she is not interested in pursuing relationships: "I don't care about any of that, one way or the other. I hate sex, too—that was a big disappointment."

hate talking to pretty much everybody. Like now, I still hate talking to you, but I'm still trying to be polite."

HURTING HERSELF

At times she acted on her thoughts about death and dying, Julia says. When she was twelve, she began fantasizing about her own suicide.

"I started out by just hurting myself a lot," she says, sighing. "I'd stab myself with pencils and pens, or make marks on my arms and hands with forks or knives. Then when I was a little older, I just had this idea that I was going to die. I felt like that would be the best way. It didn't scare me or anything, it was like saying, 'Maybe I'll go outside now,' or 'Maybe I'll have a glass of juice.' It was simple like that.

"I thought it would be pretty easy, just take a bunch of pills. I'd go to sleep and never wake up. That was what I did, too. Except I didn't do it right. I didn't have the right kind of pills. I took like everything that was in the medicine cabinet, but it was mostly like vitamins and aspirin and stuff. There were a lot of pills, but obviously I didn't die. I just threw up a bunch of times and felt bad. I didn't tell nobody, either."

Julia says that after her suicide attempt, she was relieved that she had not gone through with it.

"It wasn't like I wanted to live all of a sudden," she says. "It's just that I got this flash that what if they took my dead body to some school or something for doctors. They'd be poking me, studying my body, figuring me all out. I didn't want that. And I'm glad I didn't go to no hospital, either, because they would have done the same thing to me alive. I don't want nobody coming in, taking my temperature, and listening to see if my heart is beating the right way."

"I HAD FUN THEN"

It is hard to listen to Julia talk without feeling sad for her; her life seems to her so completely pointless and dreary. Has she ever had fun—ever done things that she truly enjoyed?

"Yes, I did have one time," she says, nodding. "It was with my church, Mount Zion. I had fun then. A bunch of us were in this Praise Band together, kind of a youth group that played and danced and sang. We used to perform a lot, too, 'cause we was

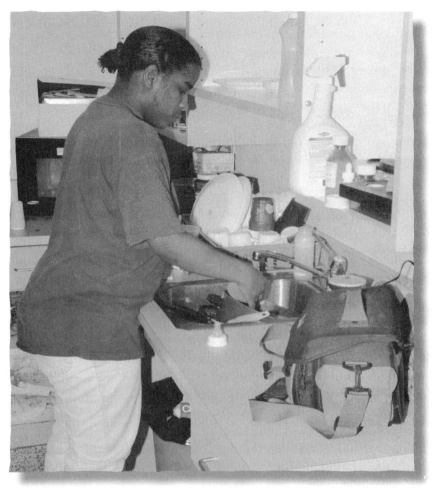

Julia has contemplated suicide many times, but what stops her is the thought of doctors "poking me, studying my body, figuring me all out."

really good. We went to youth rallies, you know, like at Bethel College. That one lasted three days. Or retreats for other churches. People really got going when we started—we sang real good."

Julia's voice has become lighter and more animated; even her expression has transformed itself to one of enthusiasm and excitement.

"We had these really nice costumes that the youth pastor's wife made. You could choose your own colors, whatever two you wanted, as long as you didn't have the same ones as someone else. My costume was red and orange—shorts and a decorated shirt. We looked really colorful—one other girl had orange and blue, one had blue and yellow, like that.

"Our best song was that one that goes, you know, dum da da da da?" she says, humming a measure. "That's 'I Love Jesus'—it's a real favorite with everybody. We even made an audio tape of it. And one time, at a college we went to, somebody videotaped our performance. It's in storage right now, while we got nowhere to live."

"It Fizzled Out"

Julia says that that was the only time in her life she ever had a real friend, too.

"Her name was Kristi, and she was older than me," she says, almost grinning. "I was thirteen, she was twenty-seven. She was one of the lead singers in the Praise Band. I wasn't her friend right away, no—in fact, I was going to fight her! I had been beating up on this boy at church, and she broke it up. I was mad at her that she was interfering, because this boy needed to get whupped.

"But Kristi was nice and right after that we started talking. She was a youth counselor at the church, so she talked to lots of people, but I know she liked me a lot. More a friend than a counselor, you know? I didn't talk to her about my mad feelings or my depression. See, when I was with Kristi, I was having fun, and I didn't want to think about that sad stuff. So I just had fun, laughed at stuff she said. We had a good time, me and Kristi."

Her voice suddenly loses its lilt; Julia's face returns to its mask of indifference.

"It fizzled out, that Praise Band," she says, yawning. "It was sort of one thing after another. First we couldn't use the youth room at the church no more, I don't remember why. And then I started having sex and messing up like that. I wasn't going to practices like I should. And then the pastor had an affair with one of the singers. After that, the drummer got a girl pregnant. I don't know, everybody started having babies, stuff like that. It just got messed up."

Running Away

Julia has retreated inside herself once more, and she explains that after the end of Praise Band, she began a period of running away.

"I'd do it a lot, just run. I mean, I didn't have a plan, didn't take no suitcase or nothing, at least not at first. I just would walk, walk anywhere, just keep going. I just wanted to get away from anything that I like recognized, you know. I didn't want to see nobody that would talk to me.

"My dad—he used to report me, file runaway reports with the police, but I figured, so what? I'd come back after a while because I didn't have no money, no place to stay. Then I'd get home and my brothers and sisters would be all like, 'Where were you? We were worried about you!' That's exactly the reason I left in the first place, I was thinking to myself.

"Anyway, I ran one time all the way back to Chicago. That's what kind of started the trouble I got in later. But anyway, the reason I ran away was because of my oldest brother, Darren. He was back in Chicago with his wife and kids. Darren was having some of the same problems I was having—just feeling sad and mad all the time. In fact, the doctors there put him on Prozac, I think."

LIVING ON THE STREETS

"Maybe it's like some genetic thing—I didn't think of that until now. I mean, he was doing the same stuff I was doing, just sleeping, not being interested in anything. And I felt like going to see what was up with him, so I left on the bus. I stayed like two weeks with him, but really, it was so depressing being around there that I left. I guess I thought when I was back home that it would better in Chicago, getting away from all my family and their chattering. I felt like I was going to explode or something. But it was just as bad in Chicago."

Julia says even though she left her brother's house, she was not ready to return home.

"I just was living on the streets—did that for about six months," she shrugs. "I didn't have too much trouble. I didn't have no money, but that's not too hard to solve. There's lots of these car wash places around there that would let people work for cash, like thirteen dollars a day. I just washed the towels that they use, and I had money for food and stuff.

"Plus, I could stay free in any old abandoned house that I found, and there were lots of those. Just find someplace, an old crack house, that's been boarded up. You just yank off one of them boards and go in and sleep. Not too clean, but at least you're out of the weather."

By the end of six months, however, Julia was ready to come home. She had not conquered her depression, though, and was as sad and angry as before, despite the isolation she experienced on the streets.

"I got hold of my mom on the phone, and she sent for me," says Julia. "She told me to come home, and that's what I did. Things didn't end up good, though. I was glad to see her and everything— I know she loves me. But I hadn't changed; in fact, my angry moods were getting worse. It didn't take her very long to find that out, either."

"So I Hit Him with a Flower Pot"

Soon after her return home, Julia got into trouble with the police. "I got into a fight with this stupid boy," she complains. "I chased him down the street with a knife, and I got caught by the police. See, this boy was so stupid, and he was always in your face saying gross, stupid things. He wasn't anybody, just one of my brother's friends. He was always acting dumb, always talking, trying to get a reaction out of you. He was telling me things like it was important to eat fruit because then when you go to the bathroom, your stool smells good. I mean, what an ass.

"I told him to leave and he wouldn't. I got really mad—he was stupid, you could tell that just by looking at him. And he just

Julia searches through a drawer for bus passes as her mother and a friend look on. Julia has been diagnosed as depressed but is fed up with therapy: "I'm not just going to talk the depression out of me."

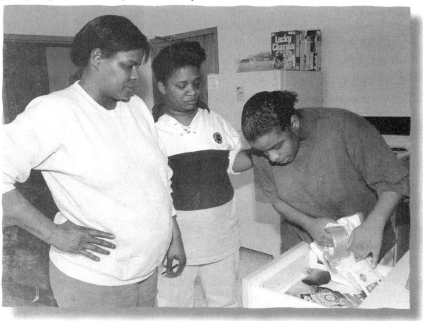

wouldn't stop talking. So I hit him with a flower pot, and I went into the house. I told him that when I came back out, he better be gone."

Julia rolls her eyes. "So, stupid as he is, he goes right out the front door and runs around the side of the house and comes in the back door. So I started hitting him in the face, and he fought me back. See this?"

She shows some dark scars on the side of her jaw. "He did that to me. I grabbed a bread knife, and I started after him. I almost had him, too, but my sister told him to run while I was getting the knife. The neighborhood watch people on the block called 9-1-1, and the police came."

INTO THE SYSTEM

Julia says that she was taken downtown to a detention center for juveniles and booked.

"I stayed there four days," she says quietly. "I hated that, too. Because I had chased him with a knife, that was worse, so it was booked as a felony. That made it more serious, yeah.

"The thing is, nobody asked me why I did it. They never talked to me or even acted interested in why I got mad. If they had, maybe that would have made them feel less sorry for that stupid boy. God, he was dumb. Anyway, I talked to the judge—it wasn't like a regular trial like on television or nothing. My sentence was that I had to do five Saturdays of community service, and I had to have a psychological evaluation."

Despite the lenient punishment, Julia did not fulfill her obligations, she says.

"I was supposed to be picking up trash on the highway," she explains. "I didn't want to do it. I mean, it wasn't really nothing, but I didn't want to do it. But they didn't like that, and so they put out a warrant for my arrest—that's what they do in those situations."

THE EVALUATION

Although she had not done the work detail on time, Julia did follow through on the judge's order for a psychological evaluation. It was there that she learned she was clinically depressed.

"I was diagnosed then," she says. "They asked me questions, lots of them. Like, what do you think about when you lie there, how long have you felt this way, what kinds of things make you feel angry—stuff like that. Then they wrote out a prescription for Prozac for me.

"No, it didn't do nothing for me. I didn't feel better, or calmer, or whatever. In fact, it made me angrier just because they were making me take that stuff, and I didn't want to. So I stopped. I guess I didn't want to get better, I don't know.

"I've seen lots of therapists and stuff since then—more than I ever wanted to. The thing is, just because someone is a therapist doesn't mean they're any smarter than anyone else. This one guy made me really mad. He was a psychiatrist, and that's like a doctor, but you'd never know it. He acted really weird, making strange expressions with his face. He asked me all these questions, just wanted to talk, talk, talk. Man, it wasn't helping, though.

"I told him, 'I don't know what you're doing—I'm not just going to talk the depression out of me.' And he wasn't getting anywhere with that talk, either. It seemed like he had the problem more than I did, if you want to know. He seemed more confused than I did. I think men just don't get it."

"Oh, I Hate Him!"

What about the young man who is the father of her baby? Does she have some semblance of relationship with him? Julia gets more animated, in an obviously negative way.

"He's nobody," she states firmly. "I hate him so much I can't even tell you. Oh, I hate him! I don't even want to talk about him, but I will for a minute. I met him a couple of years ago when I came back from Chicago. He was over at my sister's house. He was a friend of her husband, and a complete idiot."

She shakes her head and grimaces. "Oh, I'd forgotten how much I hate the father of my baby. What does he do—is that what you want to know? I'll tell you, he has a job—it's just an illegal one. He sells crack.

"I met him at the beginning of last year. I had come back from Chicago after running away, remember that? Anyway, this guy's name was Harold. He's older than me, too. I'm seventeen, and he's twenty-nine—twelve years older. I'll say he got me pregnant; I refuse to say we had a more meaningful relationship. It was no relationship. I wasn't a virgin then; I'd had sex back when I was thirteen.

"So I come up pregnant, and I told my older sister first. I wasn't real angry or nothing, I just figured it was something else happening to me. Anyway, my older sister helped me tell my mom. And she was pretty good about it, didn't get mad.

"Then Harold noticed I was a little different-acting towards him, and asked if I was pregnant. He should have some experience—he's got five kids already! I say he's got five kids, but I didn't say he acted like a father to any of them. I don't care, either. It was my pregnancy; I didn't worry about what he thought or didn't think about it."

"I Go Get Her and Hold Her and Look at Her"

Julia says her pregnancy was normal; she had all the support she needed from her family.

"I didn't need Harold, that's for sure," she says sarcastically. "It's a good thing, too, 'cause he wouldn't have been too good about giving me nothing. I mean, he was sort of interested that I was having this baby, but you know, two days after Alize was born, he's asking things like 'Are you sure it's my baby?' Interesting, huh?"

Asked how she chose the name Alize for her newborn daughter, Julia smiles almost shyly.

Julia does not mind caring for her small baby without the help of her baby's father. "I didn't need Harold, that's for sure. . . . It's a good thing, too, 'cause he wouldn't have been too good about giving me nothing."

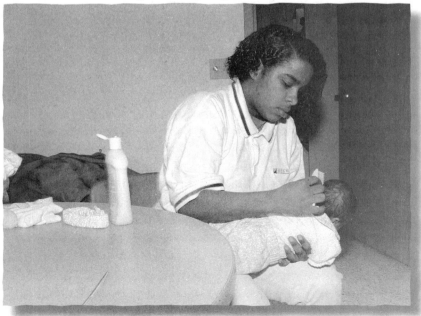

"It's a pretty name, huh? Well, it's from a song by Tupac Shakur—you know, the rapper that got killed? I guess it sounds kind of silly, but I'm in love with him, I guess. He's just someone I love everything about—his music, his body, his voice, everything. So on this one CD, there's this song where he talks about Alize. I thought it was such a pretty name. It's actually a kind of slang word for liquor, you know, but it's pretty even so.

"So Alize is my world now. She's two months old and really pretty. I figure she's kind of a lifeline for me. When I get depressed, which I do a lot, I go get her and hold her and look at her. She's the reason I can't do what I was doing no more. I can't be all inside myself all the time when I've got a baby girl, that isn't right. So I'm trying hard."

She sighs again, looking slightly overwhelmed. "My mother helps me a lot; she's always asking to babysit her. She's always saying, 'You know, Julia, you can get out if you want to, go out with your friends. I can take care of this baby.' But I don't want to go out with friends. I never did before. Now I got me a good excuse to just say no thank you."

"I GET SO MAD, SO SAD"

Julia says that although Alize has helped her feel less depressed, she still has very definite opinions on other people's behavior.

"One thing that never used to make me so sad is all the bad news about people killing their kids," she says, shuddering. "I never really thought about it much, not like now. I hear these stories, like the girl who had a baby and she and her boyfriend killed it, or the girl who had a baby at her prom and stuck it in a garbage can. I get so mad, so sad."

Asked whether she thinks such acts are done by people who are mentally ill, she shrugs.

"Who cares if they are?" she sniffs. "I think they're just evil; they're possessed. I've got a mental illness, but I'd never do that to Alize. I couldn't even think of doing that to a little baby!

"There's another thing, too—the way men act," she continues without a pause. "I hate those games they play. Like, there's this one guy at the shelter. He's here with his wife and everything, but don't you think he's flirting with me every day? I really hate him, and he's very ugly. Goodness, you should see him. I thought about telling one of the workers here, but I don't want to cause no trouble for his wife. So that's another reason that I stay upstairs in my room, away from everyone I don't know.

"See that's the thing about being homeless. You have to depend on other people. That's okay, but you don't get to be private. Here, there's all sorts of people around, same as anywhere. But when it's not your own place, you can't throw all them out like you could at your own house. The good thing is, we aren't going to be here for that much longer. We're going to be out of here in less than a week, I hope. We're just waiting for another place to be available, so we won't be having these same problems all the time. But like I said, for now it's bad.

"There's another lady who works here at the shelter, Joyce. She's kind of retarded, but I don't feel sorry for her even though I probably should. She has an attitude problem about the people here, like she's better than them. I told her she's stupid, and I threatened her. Another lady here told me that Joyce is just slow and to ignore her remarks. But I don't think that's right. I think Joyce needs to learn to shut her mouth or someone's going to shut it for her—like me, for instance."

Julia is unsure of the prognosis of her depression. She knows that she should be on medication, but knows also that it does not work as well as it should. Her impatience with doctors and psychologists makes it difficult for her to benefit from therapy.

"I don't need none of that," she says irritably. "I told you, I got Alize. And I got other ways of staying balanced out with my moods. Like, I listen to my music; that usually helps me.

"Tupac Shakur, like I said, he's best. When he died, I cried a long time. I found out about it when I was having a depressed time; I was in bed and the radio was on. That man was fine—you can always tell by looking at his eyes. And really, I heard that he's not even dead."

ALIVE IN CUBA

Realizing that perhaps she is not being taken seriously, Julia blushes.

"No, really, he's not dead. They've found him down in Cuba. They staged the death to keep him safe. That's what they said on the radio. See, he was being threatened, so to make sure he was out of harm's way, they staged it all—but it's just a cover. That's good, I say. He'll be back singing maybe, but under a different name with a disguise or something. I'm happy about that.

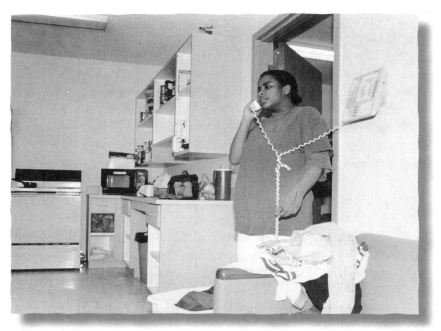

Julia has dreams, but so far they are vague. "Maybe I'd work as a social worker or a financial worker."

"The thing is, a lot of people make me mad. They say his music is all killing and violence and disrespectful of women. I saw one talk show—Jenny Jones, I think—and the whole show was about him and his music. It made me so mad! These little girls were standing up talking about how he talks about women, like in that song 'You Wonder Why They Call You Bitch.' They were saying that he's talking about all women, but that isn't true at all. He's talking about the ones who are after the money, after the things they can use. That's all."

This said, she takes a deep breath. "It's music, after all. He's got a right to rap about whatever he wants to. And the way I think, he's made lots of money off it, so it must have been good, right? Anyway, listening to him makes me feel better. And when I get some money for raising this child from Harold, that will make me feel better, too.

"See, he's fighting his paternity in court. But he's the baby's father. I know that, and Harold knows that, too. But he's being stupid about it, and it's going to be a whole lot worse for him. Because I was under age when I got pregnant, they can go after him for statutory rape. It's too bad. I mean, I don't care about that part—I just wanted some support from him. And if he'd taken care of his responsibilities, we could have avoided all this.

"As for now, I'm just going one day at a time. I can't think about no future. I never did, even when I was younger. Sometimes I think I don't want to be on welfare like my mom was. I think about getting a job—a good one that would be fun. Maybe I'd work as a social worker or a financial worker. Man, they need them—none of those people has a clue. And they don't know how to treat poor people with any respect at all.

"So I know I could do that. But I don't know how much school you have to do for that. Sometimes I get depressed about things still. I try to talk to myself, tell myself it isn't that important. And I think about Alize, and she helps me a lot. But I know I got a long way to go."

Epilogue

In the months since the four young people in this book were interviewed, there have been some changes in their lives. Although Nathan had hoped to return to a regular high school this fall, his parents decided to homeschool him one more year. He was just invited to homecoming at the high school by a girl he has known since seventh grade, and he is excited about that. Basketball will begin for him in just a few weeks, says Nathan, "so I'll have more to do with kids my own age."

Runa was ecstatic about leaving for college. "I've already talked on the phone to my new roommate," she says, "and we've gotten to know each other pretty well. I think this is going to be a big step for me, but I just know things will turn out great."

Things have not turned out as well for Ryan. Although his aunt and uncle left for Utah, Ryan was not able to go with them on the bus. A day before they were scheduled to leave, he got into a fight with one of his cousins and the police were called. He was taken to the Juvenile Corrections Center and, after being evaluated as a drug user, was transported to a local treatment center. His mother has not heard from him in a long time, she says, and has no idea how long he will be confined.

Julia and her daughter have moved from the shelter, but she left no forwarding address.

Places to Write for More Information

THE FOLLOWING ORGANIZATIONS CAN BE CONTACTED FOR ADDITIONAL INFORMATION ABOUT DEPRESSION AND BIPOLAR DISORDER.

American Association for Marriage and Family Therapy
1100 17th St. NW, 10th Fl.
Washington, DC 20036-4601
This professional organization is made up of both family and adolescent therapists throughout the United States and Canada. Readers can send a letter requesting a list of clinical members in their local area.

American Psychiatric Association (APA)
Division of Public Affairs
1400 K St. NW
Washington, DC 20005
The APA offers written material to people interested in learning about mental illness, including various forms of depression.

Depression and Related Affective Disorders Association
Johns Hopkins University, School of Medicine
Meyer 3-81
600 N. Wolfe St.
Baltimore, MD 21205
This nonprofit organization provides support and education for people with depression or related mental disorders.

National Foundation for Depressive Illness, Inc. (NFDI)
PO Box 2257
New York, NY 10116
(800) 248-4344
Interested people can call the toll-free number to get a recorded message describing the symptoms of depression and bipolar disorder as well as instructions on how to receive additional information. The NFDI also provides a bibliography and other written information about depression.

For Further Reading

Margaret Backman, *Coping with Choosing a Therapist.* New York: Rosen Group, 1994. Although this book primarily deals with questions adolescents have when choosing a therapist for a range of psychological issues, it contains good background material on depression, in addition to a good bibliography.

Harris Clemes and Reynold Been, *How to Raise Children's Self-Esteem.* Los Angeles: Price Stern Sloan, 1990. This book is written for parents, but it contains valuable information about some of the early causes of childhood depression.

Colette Dowling, *You Mean I Don't Have to Feel This Way? New Help for Depression, Anxiety, and Addiction.* New York: Scribner's, 1991. This book is written for an adult audience; however, there is a good chapter about depression affecting teens and younger children.

Judith Galas, *Teen Suicide.* San Diego: Lucent Books, 1994. Written for teens, this book presents an overview of the problem of teen suicide and offers probable causes and means of prevention.

Lawrence L. Kems, *Helping Your Depressed Child: A Reassuring Guide to the Causes and Treatments of Childhood and Adolescent Depression.* Rocklin, CA: Prima Publishing, 1993. In addition to providing an excellent, chapter-by-chapter bibliography, this book provides positive answers to questions many teens might have about the treatment of depression.

Beth Wilkinson, *Drugs and Depression.* New York: Rosen Group, 1994. This easy-to-read book shows the link between adolescent depression and drug and alcohol use.

Index

ABOUT THE AUTHOR

Gail B. Stewart is the author of more than eighty books for children and young adults. She lives in Minneapolis, Minnesota, with her husband, Carl, and their sons, Ted, Elliot, and Flynn. When she is not writing, she spends her time reading, walking, and watching her sons play soccer.

Although she has enjoyed working on each of her books, she says that *The Other America* series has been especially gratifying. "So many of my past books have involved extensive research," she says, "but most of it has been library work—journals, magazines, books. But for these books, the main research has been very human. Spending the day with a little girl who has AIDS, or having lunch in a soup kitchen with a homeless man—these kinds of things give you insight that a library alone just can't match."

Stewart hopes that readers of this series will experience some of the same insights—perhaps even being motivated to use some of the suggestions at the end of each book to become involved with someone of the Other America.

ABOUT THE PHOTOGRAPHER

Twenty-two-year-old Theodore E. Roseen currently attends Hamline University in St. Paul, Minnesota, and is studying secondary education in social studies. He has been a photographer for the university's student newspaper, *The Oracle*, for more than three years.